Shakespeare
by Jean Paris

Contents

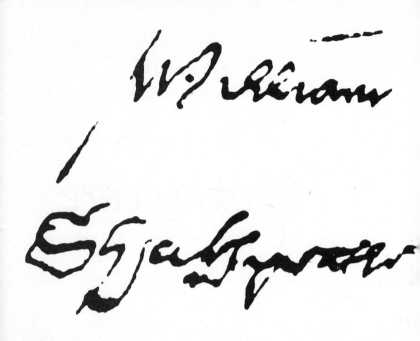

First published in This Edition 1960. All Rights Reserved.

Library of Congress Catalog Card Number: 59-10789

Evergreen Profile Books are published

in the United States by Barney Rosset at Grove Press Inc.

64 University Place   New York 3, N.Y.

in Great Britain by Evergreen Books, Ltd.

17 Sackville Street   London, W. 1

Distributed in Canada by McClelland & Stewart Ltd., 25 Hollinger Rd., Toronto 16

First published in France by Editions du Seuil, Paris

MANUFACTURED BY MOUTON & Co., IN THE NETHERLANDS

JEAN PARIS

Translated by Richard Seaver

Shakespeare

Evergreen Profile Book 10

GROVE PRESS, INC. EVERGREEN BOOKS, LTD.
NEW YORK LONDON

Chronology

1533   September 7th: Elizabeth, the daughter of Henry VIII and Anne Boleyn, is born at Greenwich.

1558   François de Guise recaptures Calais from the English. On November 17th the death of Mary Tudor brings to an end the persecutions against the Protestants.

1559   Elizabeth is crowned Queen in London on January 15th in an atmosphere of festive gaiety. April 3rd: the treaty of Cateau-Cambrésis.

1564   April 23rd: the birth of William Shakespeare at Stratford-on-Avon.

1565   July 29th: Mary Stuart, the daughter of James V of Scotland, marries young Lord Darnley at Holyrood.

1566   The birth at Edinburgh of James VI of Scotland, the future King of England.

1567   The birth of Robert Devereux, the Second Earl of Essex. On the night of February 8-9, the Earl of Bothwell assassinates Darnley at Kirk O'Field.

1570   Pope Pius V excommunicates Elizabeth. The Lord Mayor of London forbids actors from performing within the city limits.

1572   The revolt of the Low Countries against Philip II. On August 25th, the Court goes into mourning on learning of the massacre of the Protestants on St. Bartholomew's Eve.

5

Laurence Olivier in Richard III.

Elizabeth:
the reasons of State.

1576   James Burbage constructs the first London theatre at Shoreditch.

1577   Francis Drake undertakes his voyage around the world, stopping to rob the Spanish treasuries in Chile and Peru along the way.

1579   The publication of John Lyly's *Euphues* and Edmund Spenser's *Shepherd's Calendar*. Sir Philip Sydney composes his *Arcadia*.

1586   Leicester commands the English expeditionary corps in Holland. The death of Philip Sydney at the battle of Zutphen. A prisoner in England since 1568, Mary Stuart is accused of conspiring against the Queen and is condemned to death. The first performance of Thomas Kyd's *Spanish Tragedy*.

1587   February 8th: Mary Stuart is executed at Fotheringay.

1588   The end of July: the destruction of the Spanish Armada. The death of the Earl of Leicester on August 18th. First performance of Marlowe's *Doctor Faustus*.

1589   Essex's expedition to Portugal.

1593   Francis Bacon enters the House of Commons. In his *The Laws of Ecclesiastic Polity*, Richard Hooker fortifies the position of the Anglican Church. May 30th: the death of Christopher Marlowe.

1595   Ireland revolts.

1596   Essex and Drake raid Cadiz.

1597   Publication of Bacon's *Essays*. The actors of the Pembroke having

Mary Stuart:
reasons of the heart.

staged what was considered a seditious comedy, the Privy Council orders the theatres closed and has Ben Jonson imprisoned.

1599 July: opening of the Globe theatre. In the autum, William Stanley, the Earl of Derby, reconstitutes the acting troupe known as the 'Children of St. Paul.'

1600 Mountjoy lands in Ireland with 20,000 men.

1601 Essex's conspiracy. February 7th: the performance of *Richard II* at the Globe. February 8th: the plot fails. February 25th: Essex executed.

1602 The bloody suppression of Ireland.

1603 March 24th: the death of Elizabeth; James I crowned King.

1604 The historian Camden names Shakespeare as one of the great geniuses of his age.

1605 The famous Gunpowder Plot by the Catholics to blow up Parliament. Bacon's *The Advancement of Learning* published and presented to the king. First performance of Ben Jonson's *Volpone*.

1611 King James version of the Bible. Performance of Webster's *The White Devil*.

1613 The Globe Theatre completely destroyed by fire.

1616 April 23rd: the death of Shakespeare.

1623 Publication of *The First Folio* by John Heminge and Henry Condell.

1642 The triumphant Puritans succeed in closing the theatres.

Mr. WILLIAM

SHAKESPEARES

COMEDIES,
HISTORIES, &
TRAGEDIES.

Published according to the True Originall Copies.

LONDON
Printed by Isaac Iaggard, and Ed. Blount. 1623.

*Heavy matters! heavy matters! but look thee
here, boy. Now bless thyself: thou mettest with
things dying, I with things new born.*

The Winter's Tale[1]

The Metamorphosis

There is more to the Renaissance than historians generally lead
us to believe. It was not merely that age of transition which,
according to some, began with Columbus' discovery of America
or, as others would have it, with the wars in Italy. Nor does it fit
neatly into the dates we use to mark its beginning and end, for it
expressed a metamorphosis, a time when the world was in a state
of constant renewal. More exactly, it designated a transmutation
of society similar to that which the alchemists were imposing
on matter. Divine or terrestrial, it everywhere proclaimed the
revival of a spirit supposedly lost. Thus it presupposed an
acquaintance with death, with the forces of darkness and corruption, as well as a glorious accession to light. And of the thousands
of works it was destined to inspire, none gives a better picture
of this double truth than do Shakespeare's plays.

The accession of the Tudors to the throne in 1485 brought to
an end the Wars of Roses that for thirty years had been bleeding

---

[1] The edition of Shakespeare's works used throughout is *The Complete
Works of William Shakespeare*, edited by W. J. Craig, Oxford University
Press, 1947.

9

First edition: the folio of 1623.

the rival houses of York and Lancaster. The resulting peace, which Shakespeare extols at the end of *Richard III*, also marks the turning point in English history when the feudal age gives way to the monarchy. To be sure, Henry VII, who united the Roses by marrying Elizabeth the Yorkist heiress, was constantly beset by plots from abroad and by uprisings at home led by such imposters as Perkin Warbeck and the false Earls of Warwick; Henry VIII had forcibly to thwart the intrigues of powerful dissidents and papists, while Mary Tudor's reign was literally founded on prisons and burnings at the stake; and no reign was more plagued by internal quarrels and the adventures of the rival Spanish than was Queen Elizabeth's. But each successive test of strength served to reinforce royal authority and forge the soul of a people who became increasingly aware of its privileged situation. '*Remember, sir, my liege,*' Shakespeare was to write,

> *The kings your ancestors, together with*
> *The natural bravery of your isle, which stands*
> *As Neptune's park, ribbed and paled in*
> *With rocks unscaleable and roaring waters,*
> *With sands, that will not bear your enemies' boats,*
> *But suck them up to the topmast.*

This profession of faith is echoed by history. Long divided, England at last realized that her geographical unity called for a corresponding political unity. Faced with increasing perils from abroad, she learned to settle her domestic differences and to arm herself against any outside aggressor. Thus slowly, through wars and work, voyages and discoveries, was born this will for power that was to culminate in England's victory over Philip II's mighty armada:

> *With shame –*
> *The first that ever touch'd him – he was carried*
> *From off our coast, twice beaten; and his shipping –*
> *Poor ignorant baubles! – on our terrible seas,*
> *Like egg-shells mov'd upon their surges, crack'd*
> *As easily 'gainst our rocks...* [1]

In the realm of economics, this steadfastness of purpose enabled England to evolve from a medieval, urban stage of development

---

[1] *Cymbeline*, III, 1, 16–22; 24–29.

The attack of the Spanish Armada.

to the national stage characteristic of modern times. In a hundred years the fever already at work on the Continent would reach, infect, conquer '*this scepter'd isle*'. But at the time the houses of Lancaster and York made their peace, England found itself in much the same relationship to Flanders that France was to Italy. Like Venice and Florence, Antwerp and Bruges had become capitals of the new era: science, industry, and commerce held in their hands the nascent fortunes of the Western world. And it was to these capitals, to these fertile lands that England first went for knowledge and instruction. She proved an apt pupil and ended by surpassing those whose methods and skills she had appropriated.

By the time of Henry VIII, England was already a formidable competitor. New inventions were continually being made, giving her the means to assure her superiority. The English textile industry was mechanized and production increased rapidly. Certain regions specialized in cropping and weaving. Cambridge became a center for knitting; Bristol, Norwich, and Leicester specialized in spinning; and as Lemster's woollen serges competed on the market with Flemish cloth, English silks, linens, lace, and velvet invaded the cities of the Continent. The English metal industry underwent a similar expansion. The mining and manufacture of various metals – zinc, lead, bronze, pewter – were developed. Newcastle and Sheffield abandoned the use of charcoal in the manufacture of metal goods and replaced it with coal. At the same time the development of machines for lifting and for transportation facilitated the distribution of the finished products. Roads were improved, thus bringing the various provinces closer together. And in every part of the country new buildings were being constructed. The brick kilns worked constantly to keep up with the demand, and it was the brick which set the style for the architecture of the times, of which the masterpiece is Hampton Court Palace. Clockmaking, chemistry, glassmaking, all were affected by this technical revolution. The whole of England became an arsenal, its crowded warehouses simply waiting for outlets.

The whole foreign policy of the Tudors was to make sure there were enough markets for English goods to avoid an economic crisis. In order to keep English products flowing abroad, Henry VIII signed numerous trade agreements with the Italians, imposed duties on French wines and pastels, and greatly stepped up the English shipbuilding program. While English fishing fleets plowed the north seas, English men o' war followed close behind, and the coastal shipyards worked mightily to provide the nation with the most powerful navy in the world. From the modest figure of 42, the number of ships registered in Queen Elizabeth's time rose to an amazing 1,232, and this supremacy is exemplified by the expeditions of Drake, Davis, Frobisher, Cavendish, and others...

> *Your mind is tossing on the ocean;*
> *There, where your argosies with portly sail, –*
> *Like signiors and rich burghers on the flood,*
> *Or, as it were, the pageants of the sea, –*
> *Do overpeer the petty traffickers,*
> *That curtsy to them, do them reverence,*
> *As they fly by them with their woven wings.*[1]

Not the least of capitalism's failings is that it demands, from its very inception, an expansion of this sort. The demand grows proportionately as wealth increases. Whence blows this wind of

London: bourgeois dress.

---
[1] *The Merchant of Venice*, I, 1, 8–14.

which Shakespeare speaks '*that scatters young men through the world to seek their fortunes further than at home*'. With the need to protect distant possessions, establish foreign banks, gain control of key positions throughout the world, was born the age of voyages. Similarly, the necessity of conquering virgin territories, of exploiting their natural resources, of prospering at their expense, led inevitably to colonialism, with Spain setting the most flagrant example. The need to enslave the natives and bend them to the most abject labor, to buy and sell them like cattle, resulted in the ineradicable shame of the age, sanctified by Hawkins and Drake: the Negro slave traffic.

The result of this prodigious development is easy to predict: the amassing of prodigious fortunes. Manufacturers, contractors, businessmen, slave traders, arms manufacturers, bankers, traders – all grown rich together – formed a new class with whom the king quickly learned to come to terms.

> *Pisa, renowned for grave citizens,*
> *Gave me my being and my father first,*
> *A merchant of great traffic through the world,*
> *Vincentio, come of the Bentivolii.*

In Tudor England this new class of self-made men became increasingly powerful, and with them was born the positive spirit, a harsh, uncompromising attitude toward the poor, and a thirst for profit, luxury, and pleasure.

> *First, as you know, my house within the city*
> *Is richly furnished with plate and gold:*
> *Basins and ewers to lave her dainty hands;*
> *My hangings all of Tyrian tapestry;*
> *In ivory coffers I have stuff'd my crowns;*
> *In cypress chests my arras counterpoints,*
> *Costly apparel, tents, and canopies,*
> *Fine linen, Turkey cushions boss'd with pearl,*
> *Valance of Venice gold in needle-work,*
> *Pewter and brass, and all things that belong*
> *To house or housekeeping: then, at my farm*
> *I have a hundred milch-kine to the pail,*
> *Six score fat oxen standing in my stalls,*
> *And all things answerable to this portion.*[1]

---

[1] *The Taming of the Shrew*, I, 1, 10–13; II, 1, 339–353.

14

The 'Good Queen Bess': a portrait of power.

As the owners of these goods, this new merchant class owned everything. The Wars of the Roses, which had just decimated the military aristocracy, paved the way for their speculations. They quickly expanded their sphere of influence, made loans to the king, the state, the clergy, as well as to the lower classes; they founded colonies, subsidized voyages of exploration, set up monopolies, and took over the estates formerly owned by the nobility. As if anxious to see them a part of the government, Henry VIII looked with a favorable eye on their political endeavors. The king himself appropriated his enemies' feudal estates, or taxed them unmercifully; he seized the Catholics' former holdings, closed their convents, confiscated their treasuries and, rejecting once and for all the yoke of Rome, established the ideal religion of the merchant class: the Anglican Church. His program was to be carried out point by point by his daughter Elizabeth. Throughout her reign, 'good Queen Bess' gave her support to the middle class in order to weaken the nobility, actively supported the Reformed Church and persecuted those still faithful to Rome. The Essexes

15

and Southamptons could fret and fume, Pope Pius V issue his bulls of excommunication: the simple presence of the merchant Boleyn's grand-daughter on the throne was proof enough that the real authority of the country had indeed changed hands.

> *What earthly name to interrogatories*
> *Can task the free breath of a sacred king?*
> *Thou canst not, cardinal, devise a name*
> *So slight, unworthy and ridiculous,*
> *To charge me to an answer, as the pope.*
> *Tell him this tale; and from the mouth of England*
> *Add thus much more: that no Italian priest*
> *Shall tithe or toll in our dominions.*[1]

Politically, this society rested on the absolute power of the Queen, assisted by a Privy Council, the Councils of the North, and the Gallic Marches, the Exchequer, Parliament, the Courts of Justice, and the local administrative organs. Everyone who held a government post received payment in two distinctly different ways: 'fees' or rights, which were fixed by law, and 'gratuities' or gifts, which were disbursed capriciously or through actual misappropriation of public funds. Thus the Keeper of the Seals received an official salary of £919, but unofficially received £3,000; the Lord Admiral a trifle more, the First Secretary a little less. From the top of the hierarchy to the bottom, what really counted was the extent of one's favor or influence with the Court: the taxes one paid, personal patronages received or honors granted, payment for services rendered, charters, licenses, monopolies, profits. Thus there grew up between the Queen and her petitioners a plethora of intermediaries who either had to be supplanted or won over. Anyone looking for a favor had to pay for it; and subsequently everyone had his price. Upon the death of Lord Burghley, long the Queen's most trusted adviser and certainly one of the least corrupt dignitaries of the Court, the inventory of his possessions revealed that between January, 1596 and August, 1598 he had extorted £3,103 6s. 8d. from eleven different people. In certain families, the major-domos were given only their food and lodging, with tips and bribes accounting for their real income. These malpractices, which were rife in all levels of society, led to the formation of various

---

[1] *King John*, III, 1, 77–81.

16

A plethora of intermediaries...

desperate and ambitious groups intent on gaining control of the state machinery. Hence the dissensions and collusions of such men as Leicester, Cecil, Essex, and Raleigh. Elizabeth, kept fully informed of these rivalries by her network of spies and counterspies, only managed to govern by maintaining a precarious balance among the vying factions, either by favoring first one and then another, or by doing away with anyone whose prestige or demands seemed excessive or dangerous. And was it not this state of affairs which prompted Shakespeare to write these well-known, indignant lines?

POSVI DEVM ADIVTOREM MEVM

SEMPER EADEM

ELISABET D.G. ANGLIAE, FRANCIAE, HIBERNIAE, ET VERGINIAE REGINA,
FIDEI CHRISTIANAE PROPVGNATRIX ACERRIMA, NVNC IN DNO REQVIESCENS

> *Who dares, who dares,*
> *In purity of manhood stand upright,*
> *And say, 'This man's a flatterer?' if one be,*
> *So are they all; for every grize of fortune*
> *Is smooth'd by that below: the learned pate*
> *Ducks to the golden fool: all is oblique;*
> *There's nothing level in our cursed natures*
> *But direct villany.*[1]

The dangers of despotism, the rapacity of those in power, the covetousness of subalterns, the struggles among the mighty, the frailty of a glory that hovers on the brink of disgrace,

> *the whips and scorns of time,*
> *The oppressor's wrong, the proud man's contumely,*
> *The pangs of dispriz'd love, the law's delay,*
> *The insolence of office, and the spurns*
> *That patient merit of the unworthy takes...*[2]

are not all these failures and shortcomings really the subjects of Shakespeare's plays?

For a mighty drama was unfolding in this age. Together with the economic and political upheavals of the time, the world was gripped by an unprecedented spiritual crisis. Not only were the social classes undergoing profound shifts, but new concepts and knowledge were everywhere apparent; and it is precisely in this variation that Spencer and Tillyard see the origin of the Shakespearean theatre. 'One of the characteristics of the intellectual revival known as the Renaissance was the appearance of naturalist attitudes in sharp conflict with the attitudes prescribed by traditional religion.'[3]

Astronomers, theologians, and jurists of the Middle Ages had interpreted the universe, man, and society in strictly religious terms. Decreed by God, the hierarchy of values and of people derived from a cosmic order. For Saint Thomas, for Dante, the laws of the world and of reason emanated from God, and the road to salvation for all mankind was through self-fulfillment. In such an optimistic world view, evil could only exist through a denial of grace, a misplaced emphasis on unworthy values. As

---

[1] *Timon of Athens.* IV, 2, 49-56.
[2] *Hamlet*, III, 1, 70-74.
[3] Cf. H.-B. Parkes: 'Nature's diverse laws: the double vision of the Elizabethans,' in *The Sewanee Review*, LVIII, no. 3, 1950.

late as 1593 such a man as Richard Hooker could still hold firmly to these tenets: evil could only be a deviation from good, and excellence must necessarily result in all things if only they followed their true course. Nevertheless, with the dawn of the 16th century, scholars began the empirical study of nature, whose forces they suspected might be able to be controlled and utilized. Of course, they still believed that men and the cosmos were governed by analogous laws, but as time went on these laws came to be considered less and less as divinely inspired, and more and more thought of as measurable relationships, as systems independent of all ethics. Thus the Elizabethans lived in an age when the beliefs of the Middle Ages had ceased to be meaningful, while the doctrines destined to replace them had not as yet been formulated. Believing that the world was fundamentally good, that the celestial order was the guarantee of a terrestrial order, they lived in an age when neither logic nor morality tempered the thirst for power, when the exercise of authority was especially characterized by abuses. This disparity between past and future, ideal and reality, was to constitute the major theme of their works. Powerless to reconcile divine ideals with the injustice and disorder of the world around them, they had to assume these 'grating contradictions' and, moving from doubt to denial, from revolt to despair, at last proclaim the advent of Evil:

> *Ah! gracious lord, these days are dangerous.*
> *Virtue is chok'd with foul ambition,*
> *And charity chas'd hence by rancour's hand;*
> *Foul subornation is predominant,*
> *And equity exil'd your highness' land.*[1]

From 1585 to 1600 the influence of Copernicus, Montaigne, and Machiavelli brought this conflict to a climax. A Philip Sydney, an Edmund Spenser, had managed to avoid it by clothing their work in mythological trappings. It was Christopher Marlowe who first espoused a pessimistic view of existence. In his four principal plays this shoemaker's son, educated at Cambridge, servant of the Earl of Nottingham, this secret agent and moralist of genius, converted the theater into man's tribunal. *Tamburlaine*, *Doctor Faustus*, *The Jew of Malta*, and *Edward II* heralded the tragedies of Lear, Hamlet, Macbeth, and Anthony. In *Tamburlaine*, Marlowe portrays a tartar tyrant whose inordinate ambition

---

[1]   *Henry VI, Part 2*, III, 1, 141–146.

and thirst for conquest condemns him to solitude; in *Doctor Faustus*, the ominous example of pride so great it exchanges eternal salvation for a moment's knowledge. With Barrabas the knave and Edward the impotent, this quest for grandeur degenerates into the quest for vice. Depraved characters invade the stage as they invaded the Court. Those who remain untainted have barely time enough to take refuge in a Seneca-like stoicism, and already death knocks at the gates of this irremissibly lost world. The deceit of glory, science's damnation, the decay of the soul: all these are problems crying for solutions. But on May 30, 1593, Marlowe was struck down by an assassin's knife in a Deptford tavern. And to Shakespeare alone was henceforth left the task of resolving the moral tragedy of his age.

A Jansenist portrait.

The Pretenders

There are other poets as great as Shakespeare; there is none
more enigmatic. By that I mean that there is no one who today
provokes more violent discussion or raises more problems. More
than three centuries after the epilogue of *The Tempest*, every word
he wrote is still discussed, every statement he made still arouses
controversy. And as the number and variety of analyses increase,
the mystery lessens only to add to the confusion. This mystery
would first of all seem to be: how could any one man harbor such
diversity? Of the 'thousand souls' that Goethe gave him, which
one did he really incarnate? Who was he? Aristocrat, initiate,
prophet, politician, Jesuit, homosexual, usurer, misanthrope,
madman, puritan, mystic, agitator, or, as the ineffable Tolstoy
would have it, 'after all, a mediocre writer?'

For certain critics this sort of concern seems henceforth
meaningless. According to them there is no longer any 'Shakespeare
secret,' or at least such a secret is not really the one people think
it is. All the ambiguities and contradictions connected with
Shakespeare vanish the moment one ceases to believe he was the
author of the plays attributed to him. Which means? Simply
that the man from Stratford-on-Avon was nothing more than a
man of straw, the pseudonym of a genius who, for various reasons,

preferred to remain anonymous. There thus would be a pseudo-Shakespeare, as there is a pseudo-Denys, and this magic name was merely used to perpetrate a tremendous hoax. The greatest hoax ever perpetrated, to be sure, but not the only one. For this example serves to corroborate a whole tradition of imposture. Everyone knows, for instance, that Solomon was the author of the *Iliad* and Nausiçaa the author of the *Odyssey;* that the comedies of Terence, Virgil's *Aeneid* and the *Odes* of Horace were written by the monks of the Middle Ages; that Tacitus' *Annals* were forged by Poggio Bracciolini; that King Alfred wrote *Beowulf* and George III the *Letters of Junius;* that *Paradise Lost* was drafted by a group presided over by Ellwood; that Corneille wrote Molière's plays and Molière penned La Fontaine's *Fables;* that *In Memoriam* was not composed by Tennyson but by his wife; and that Madame Michelet was, similarly, the author of her husband's lyric works.

It was in 1856 that Miss Delia Bacon – who claimed no relationship with her illustrious namesake – published her now-famous article in *Putnam's Monthly* entitled 'Shakespeare and His Plays: An Enquiry Concerning Them,' which she expanded the following year into a 543-page book, *The Philosophy of the Plays of Shakespeare Unfolded.* In these she claimed that Francis Bacon[1] was

---

[1]   Actually she claimed chief authorship for Bacon, and suggested that Raleigh, Lord Buckhurst, Lord Paget, and the Earl of Oxford were also collaborators.

really the author of Shakespeare's plays. Not long after making this momentous pronouncement she retired to the sanctity of an insane asylum. But already her theory had begun to catch the fancy of other critics. In 1856 a certain William Smith declared before the Shakespeare Society that the author of *Novum Organum* and the man who had written *Macbeth* were indeed one and the same. Others soon flocked to the cause, and as early as 1883 Mrs. Pott, Ignatius Donnelly, Edwin Reed, and W. H. Burr prepared the public for the supreme discovery: the biliteral cipher of Sir Francis Bacon, deciphered by Mrs. Elizabeth Wells Gallup, showed that Sir Francis had written not only Shakespeare's plays, but also those of Marlowe, Greene, Peele, and Jonson, certain sections of Spenser's *Faerie Queene*, and Burton's *The Anatomy of Melancholy*, and, what was more, that he was the son of Queen Elizabeth by her favorite, the Earl of Leicester!

These astounding allegations were soon buttressed by an even more amazing revelation. The supernatural was injected into the debate and, through the intermediary of a Spiritualist from the New World, completely confirmed these views. To this unexpected testimony were added the minor resources of philology. Mrs. Pott made public a list of notes and quotations revealing 4,400 impressive analogies between Bacon's texts and those of the false Shakespeare. An examination of this list showed, in fact, that these analogies included such conclusive examples as: 'Good morrow', 'amen', 'I assure you', and 'believe me'. The same was true for the 230 Latin words that R. Theobald produced as proof that Shakespeare must have been a learned man: yet all these words can be found in the works of other writers of the same period, as well as in those of their predecessors. Similarly, the evidence adduced by Dr. Webb – who noted that the phrase 'discourse of reason' was used four times by Shakespeare and often by Bacon – failed to mention that this same phrase also occurs in the writings of Thomas More, in Montaigne's *Essays* and Holland's *Plutarch*. Nevertheless Webb stuck by his guns, and his 'discoveries' were frequently used by later literary hacks. Webb even went so far as to suggest that Shakespeare the poet and Shakespeare the actor were perhaps two different people. Had he forgotten the tributes of the First Folio? Certainly not. But through a fantastic interpretation of Jonson's *Ode* he concluded that old Ben was in on the secret. Besides, everyone knows that Jonson and Bacon were on such good terms that the poet collaborated on the *Novum Organum*! Finally, the most telling argument of all was brought to light by W. Smith in the postscript of a letter from Sir Tobie Matthews to Bacon, in which we read: 'The most prodigious wit that ever I knew of my nation and of this side of the sea is of your Lordship's name, though he be known by another.' Did this letter, written early in 1621, contain the long awaited proof that Shakespeare was really Bacon's pseudonym? Sidney Lee soon dashed this hope by proving that Matthews, a Roman Catholic, was referring to a Jesuit he had met on the Continent, Father Thomas Southwell, whose surname was indeed Bacon, though his first name was not Francis. And that was that.

And yet in 1592 a new candidate had been found by J. Greenstreet in the person of William Stanley, the sixth Earl of Derby. This Shakespeare was the first of a series of aristocrats, and added a notable argument to the anti-Stratford theories. For if it was difficult to understand why Bacon, who signed his own name to his philosophical treatises, should have been reluctant to sign his plays, it was quite easy to see why a claimant to the throne would want to conceal his theatrical endeavors. Thus the most wily politician of Elizabethan England was hiding behind 'the mask of Shakespeare'. M. Abel Lefranc, with his customary acumen, had suspected this fact about 1916, and thirty years of patient research were not going to make him change his mind: the poet who wrote *Love's Labour's Lost* had spent some time at the Court of Navarre; *Twelfth Night* portrayed 'scenes from one of the Derby castles'; *Hamlet* retraced the story of Mary Stuart; Stanley's well-known jealousy found its expression in *Othello*, *Troilus and Cressida*, *Cymbeline*, and *The Winter's Tale*; the 'dark period' was to be explained by Stanley's disappointment at being displaced by James I. In short, there was a strange parallelism between the Shakespearean theater and Derby's career. Two documents transformed these conjectures into virtual certainties: these were 'two letters written in June 1599 by a secret agent whose name was purported to be George Fenner'. Seized by Elizabeth's police, these missives related that the Earl was 'solely occupied with composing plays, a task which kept him, at least in appearance, from pursuing his political ventures'.[1]

Unfortunately, there are several facts which tend to refute these extraordinary deductions. There is no doubt that William Stanley had a profound interest in the theatre. But nothing, absolutely

[1] Abel LeFranc: *Discovering Shakespeare*, Paris, A. Michel, 1950, vol. II, p. viii.

nothing, attests to the fact that he encouraged Shakespeare and his friends. On the contrary, all evidence indicates that he supported their rivals. In 1599, the same year that some vague spy wrote of Stanley's theatrical pursuits, the Earl reconstituted the company known as the 'Children of St. Paul', the same troupe that Shakespeare pokes fun at in *Hamlet*. What is even more surprising for a man of such genius is the fact that he turned to John Marston's satirical repertory as a source of plays for his youthful company. Moreover, several of Stanley's letters are extant, and the most one can say for them is that their style is a far cry from that of *Macbeth* or *King Lear*. Even his life seems dull, completely taken up with petty intrigues and conjugal quarrels. Even his death argues against him. For by what strange coincidence did Stanley, who died in 1642, stop writing plays in 1616, the year of Shakespeare's death?

There is no point in commenting further on the other puppets whom various people have tried to set up as Aeschylus' equal. Roger Manners, the fifth Earl of Rutland, exhumed from oblivion by Celestin Demblon, had departed this life well before *Henry VIII*. Edward de Vere, the eighteenth Earl of Oxford, enthroned by Thomas Looney, B. M. Ward, Percy Allen, and G. Rendall, was at best a mediocre poet, who has no more claim to Shakespeare's genius than do William Cecil or Francis Walsingham. There is, moreover, one event that suffices to refute these heresies once and for all. In February 1601, the famous trial of Essex and his accomplices began in London. Accused of having conspired to overthrow the Queen, the plotters claimed that they had merely intended to rid her of her corrupt advisers. The prosecution retorted that the actors of the Globe Theatre, of whom Shakespeare was one, had each been paid 40 shillings by the conspirators to perform *Richard II*, the play they judged most likely to help overthrow Elizabeth. Among the prosecutors were none other than Bacon, Oxford, and Derby. Suppose one of them were really the author of *Richard II*; would it not have taken a singular Machiavellianism to use this play as one of the principal pieces of evidence against the conspirators? As for Rutland, he was among the accused at this trial, but he showed himself to be such an ass that the judges ruled he should not be held responsible for his actions. Thus must we subscribe wholeheartedly to the conclusions drawn by Mrs. Longworth Chambrun: 'It is curious to note that this tragic trial brought together all the "false Shakespeares", a fact which in itself is sufficient to render the four anti-Stratford theories meaningless.'[1]

Faced with this evidence, it is understandable that the die-hards came up with an even more radical hypothesis. If it seems so difficult to recreate a single Shakespeare, it is because there were, in reality, several. By this they mean that Shakespeare's name served as a signature for a whole clique of propagandists, including both members of the nobility and some artists more or less in the pay of the secret police. High up in the hierarchy of the first group were the Earl of Oxford, the son-in-law of the Prime Minister, and the Earl of Derby, Oxford's son-in-law. And chief among the second group was Christopher Marlowe.[2] A collective Shakespeare! now here was an ingenious method of reconciling all the critics. Only in this case, why the need for deceit? It is perhaps feasible that an ambitious and artful person, or that a group of conspirators, might have made use of a pseudonym. But why would those in complete agreement and favor with the Crown resort to such puerile subterfuge? And why would Derby get mixed up in something so diametrically opposed to his own interests? And how can we accept the fact that for twenty years, covering the reigns of two different monarchs, no one ever gave the plot away? To these problems scholars offer only grammatical or bibliographical answers. From one poet to the other, they observe, the same sentences, the same themes, the same methods can be found, without its being possible to say for certain where imitation ends and authenticity begins. In their recent studies of Elizabethan literature, L. R. Zocca, Rosemonde Tuve, and Mrs. Bradbrook all remind us of the following fact: the questions Shakespeare was concerned with, the solutions he offered to them – even the images he used to express them – originated less from his own genius than from a common heritage. One step further and the relationship between Shakespeare and his colleagues leads to what Chambers has called the 'total disintegration' of the man and his work. Who wrote *Titus Andronicus*? Kyd, Marlowe, and Greene. *Love's Labour's Lost*? Oxford and Derby. *All's Well That End's Well*? Shakespeare, Chapman, and Greene. *Troilus and Cressida*? Dekker and Chettle,

[1] Mrs. Longworth-Chambrun: *Shakespeare's 'Hamlet'*, Sfelt, p. 11.
[2] Abel Chevalley: 'Shakespeare and the Elizabethan Poets', in *The Elizabethan Theatre*, Les Cahiers du Sud, Paris, José Corti, 1940, p. 50.

revised and corrected by Greene and Chapman working together. *King John*? One of Peele's plays reworked, says Chambers; Marlowe's work, says Robertson. Happily, *The Merry Wives of Windsor* included at least eight phrases by Shakespeare himself. But in *Julius Caesar* we find Ben Jonson revising a play by Marlowe that Beaumont had reworked. And so on and so forth. As for the methods used to obtain these results – studies of rhyme, assonance, rhythms, preferred words, punctuation, spelling,

Francis Bacon: a portrait of the philosopher.

customary metaphors, allusions to circumstances, stage directions, abbreviations, misprints, faulty elisions – it is understandable that in the hands of specialists they produce 'conflicting results'. M. Abel Chevalley admits this quite candidly, but adds: 'It is not only in our day that amateurs are the real professionals and the professionals themselves mere traffickers.'

The record of Shakespeare's baptism.

I have night's cloak to hide me from their eyes.
Romeo and Juliet

'By Me, William Shakespeare'

William Shakespeare was born at Stratford-on-Avon on Apri 23, 1564. The parish register reveals that he was baptized on the 26th.

SIR ANDREW. *Shall we set about some revels?*
SIR TOBY. *What shall we do else? Were we not born under Taurus?*[1]

No one knows if the astrologers of the times duly celebrated this horoscope. Later on Shakespeare did not forget to sing the praises of this astrological period of good health, nor to observe that *'there is divinity in odd numbers, either in nativity, chance or death.'*[2] And, in fact, who was ever blessed by the gods with a greater gift of genius than was this man whose life rises out of obscurity to assume the proportions of a myth? The deeds and gestures of the lowest clod who lived in that period have come down to us. But by a strange quirk of fate, the greatest dramatist the world had seen since the golden age of Greece remains completely obscure for us: an unknown.

---

[1] *Twelfth Night*, I, 3, 146–149.
[2] *The Merry Wives of Windsor*, V, 1, 3–5.

31

'See Stratford and die': for four hundred years England's poets and their counterparts from abroad, as well as countless tourists and curiosity seekers, have visited this cottage which contains, besides the memory of Will himself, mementos from his life and times.

A little town of Warwickshire, Stratford-on-Avon boasted a population of about 1500 near the end of the sixteenth century. A certain John Shakespeare, the son of a Snitterfield farmer, was one of Stratford's wealthier citizens. In 1557 he had married one of the eight daughters of Robert Arden, the descendant of an old Catholic family and proprietor of Wilcot Manor. In his will Arden left his daughter 50 acres of land and some other possessions that her husband used to good advantage. It has never been clearly established whether John Shakespeare was himself a farmer; some say he was, while others claim he was a glover or tanner. Aubrey has him a butcher, and Rowe says he was a wool merchant. Whatever he was, John Shakespeare had purchased three or four houses and was well enough known to aspire to public office. His municipal career closely follows the rise and fall of his personal fortunes, concerning which biographers differ so greatly. First a beer taster, then constable, then treasurer, then alderman, he finally was named to the exalted post of bailiff in 1568. All evidence indicates that he performed his duties to the satisfaction of his fellow-townsmen until 1576, when his fortunes, for some unknown reason, began to decline.

John Shakespeare had eight children, three of whom died in infancy. Of the remaining five, there were four boys – William, Edmund, Richard, and Gilbert – and one daughter, Joan. The

absence of documents makes the childhood of the eldest Shakespeare boy a matter of pure conjecture. In all probability he entered the town grammar school when he was seven. The Tudors, patrons of science and the liberal arts, had pursued an

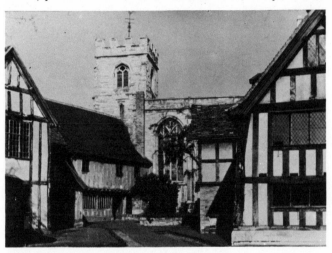

enlightened policy in matters of education and had endowed the towns and cities of England with excellent schools, whose masters were Oxford and Cambridge graduates. Four of these men – John Acton, Walter Roche, Simon Hunt, and Thomas Jenkins – succeeded one another at Stratford, where the sons of the wealthy were admitted free, thanks to the generosity of a Maecenas, Sir Hugh Clopton. Basically, the school program included the study of Latin in the work of W. Lyly and the *Sententiae Pueriles*, from which the students learned by heart numerous passages from the works of Plautus and Terence, Virgil and Ovid...

DEMETRIUS. Integer vitae, scelerisque purus
Non eget Mauri iaculis, nec arcu.

CHIRON. *O ! 'tis a verse in Horace; I know it well:
I read it in the grammar long ago.*[1]

---

[1] *Titus Andronicus*, IV, 2, 20–23.

Wilson's *Rhetoric* was used as the text for English, and the chronicles of Hall and Holinshed – from which Shakespeare later culled much of his material for the historical plays – were used to study English history. Of course we can only assume that such was Shakespeare's schooling, since there is no proof that he actually attended school. We have one slight basis for believing he did, however: his signatures reveal that he used the Gothic

calligraphy, which was the one taught at the Stratford school, and not the Italian script adopted by the universities and men of letters. And again we can only conjecture whether or not it was in the Stratford Grammar School that young Will learned the smattering of Greek that Ben Jonson claimed he knew, or the

Manuscript alleged to be Shakespeare's (Sir Thomas More).

The Stratford School.

Welsh, Italian, and French phrases with which he adorned *The Merry Wives of Windsor* and *Henry V*:

> KATHERINE: *Comment appelez-vous la main en Anglois?*
> ALICE. *La main? Elle est appelée*, de hand.
> KATHERINE. De hand. *Et... comment appelez-vous le pied et la robe?*
> ALICE. De foot, *madame, et* de coun.
> KATHERINE. De foot *et* de coun! *O Seigneur Dieu! ce sont des mots de son mauvais, corruptible, gros et impudique, et non pour les dames d'honneur d'user.*[1]

But there are other teachers who could have had a more direct influence on the formation of the child. Formerly persecuted as 'rogues and vagabonds' by the civil and religious authorities, the members of the acting profession were authorized by a decree of 1572 to form companies under the patronage of the kingdom's dignitaries. The wealthiest aristocrats sponsored these troupes, who performed for them on feast days, and the rest of the time staged their productions at provincial inns. Their means were extremely precarious, as the following passage from *A Midsummer Night's Dream* suggests:

> QUINCE. *Ay; or else one must come in with a bush of thorns and a lanthorn, and say he comes to disfigure, or present, the person of Moonshine. Then, there is another thing: we must have a wall in the great chamber; for Pyramus and Thisbe, says the story, did talk through the chink of a wall.*
> SNUG. *You can never bring in a wall. What say you, Bottom?*
> BOTTOM. *Some man or other must present Wall; and let him have some plaster, or some loam, or some rough-cast about him, to signify wall; and let him hold his fingers thus, and through that cranny shall Pyramus and Thisbe whisper.*[2]

But their tours, according to contemporary reports, drew large enough crowds to earn them the undying hatred of the Puritans. This led to an undeclared war between the supporters and detractors of the theatre, a war waged from parish to parish and in the municipal councils themselves. The anathema that such men as Thomas White and John Stockwood were to issue *ex cathedra* against the theatrical groups still did not prevent Shakes-

---

[1] *Henry V*, III, 4, 1–66. The scene is written in French.
[2] *A Midsummer Night's Dream*, III, 1, 63–76.

peare's father from being the first to offer them the use of the Stratford Town Hall. For his term of office as bailiff coincided with the visit of several important theatrical groups: the Queen's and those supported by the Earls of Leicester, Worcester, and Warwick. From all indications, therefore, young Will belonged to a family which thought highly of the theatre, and we can assume that he witnessed such scenes as those he later described in *Hamlet* and *The Taming of the Shrew:*

> POLONIUS. *The actors are come hither, my lord.*
> HAMLET. *Buzz, buzz!*
> POLONIUS. *Upon my honour, –*
> HAMLET. *Then came each actor on his ass, –*
> POLONIUS. *The best actors in the world, either for tragedy, comedy, history, pastoral, pastoral-comical, historical-pastoral, tragical-historical, tragical-comical-historical-pastoral, scene individable, or poem unlimited: Seneca cannot be too heavy, nor Plautus too light.*[1]

Not far from Stratford, moreover, the tradition of the Mystery and Morality plays – which in former times had known great popularity – was still carried on at Coventry. Originally a simple variation of the liturgy, these plays had grown more secular from the 13th to the 16th century, with the result that the clergy had first chased them from the church itself to the square in front of the church, and thence to the town proper. The various guilds took turns putting on these plays, each according to its means. Thus the goldsmiths, in *The Adoration of the Magi*, dedicated their jewels and treasures to Jesus; the bakers and winegrowers were the logical choices to perform *The Last Supper* and *The Transformation of Water to Wine;* the shipbuilders' guild constructed the ark for *The Flood*, while fishermen and fishmongers recreated the adventures of Noah and the ark. Perched on wheeled platforms, or 'pageants', as they were called, these actors traveled from place to place, and sometimes condescended to come down from their elevated stages and perform on the streets, as they did at Coventry with *Herod*. These Miracle plays became more and more secular and popular, vying with the Mystery plays for public favor. At the end of the fifteenth century the immense success of *Everyman* already attested to the vitality of the English theater. As late as 1529 it was still possible to see Studious Desire

---

[1] *Hamlet*, II, 2, 420–429.

Leicester: a portrait of the Queen's favorite.

win the child Humanity from the seductions of Sensual Appetite, in the Mystery entitled *The Four Elements*. Weaving human relationships into these entities, the plots unfolded, with cynicism or simple good-heartedness, and sometimes managed to express in the moral at the end the most rare and delicate feelings. It is impossible to insist too strongly on the thousand analogies between this esthetic and that of the Shakespearean theatre. The whole structure of his tragedies – from the fall to the redemption – is built around miracles: the denouement of *Pericles, Prince of Tyre* is only one of many examples that vividly recall the lessons of the Morality plays:

> *In Antiochus and his daughter you have heard*
> *Of monstrous lust the due and just reward:*
> *In Pericles, his queen, and daughter, seen –*
> *Although assail'd with fortune fierce and keen –*
> *Virtue preserved from fell destruction's blast,*
> *Led on by heaven, and crown'd with joy at last.*
> *In Helicanus may you well descry*
> *A figure of truth, of faith, of loyalty.*
> *In reverend Cerimon there well appears*
> *The worth that learned charity aye wears...*[1]

But to return to the realm of conjecture, one event must certainly have made a profound impression on the child's imagination. In July, 1575, Elizabeth's favorite, Robert Dudley, the Earl of Leicester, presented a magnificent festival at Kenilworth in honor of the Queen. Countless uninvited guests and hangers-on showed up for the affair. And countless biographers immediately inferred that John Shakespeare took his eldest son to see it. The cleverest among them go so far as to detect the echo of these revels in *The Tempest* and *A Midsummer Night's Dream*. Actually, however, it seems highly improbable that Shakespeare was present. But there is no doubt that he often heard people talk about it, and we may well believe that the stories he heard did awaken certain dramatic aspirations latent within him, aspirations which needed only a propitious occasion to manifest themselves.

If we take any stock in the prevailing legend, these aspirations were not long in finding an outlet: in the butcher's trade. For it was about this same time, when certain historians picture Will as carousing with some aristocratic companions, that his father's

---

[1] *Pericles*, V, 3, 85–102.

fortunes began to take a serious turn for the worse. 'Whereas he had previously contributed substantial sums to local charities and taxes' in 1577 we find him exempted from paying the poor tax and charged only a pittance for the military levy. And yet two years later he still had not paid that negligible sum. About this same time he mortgaged his wife's possessions. The following years found him involved in endless difficulties and lawsuits with his creditors – he who a few years before had been pressing his debtors. Meanwhile he had stopped coming to meetings of the corporation, and his name appears but rarely in the municipal records covering these years. In 1586 a new alderman was named in his place, 'for that Mr. Shaxspere dothe not come to the halles when they be warned nor hathe not done of longe tyme'.[1] These financial reverses explain why John Shakespeare withdrew his son from school in 1577–78 and had him bound as an apprentice, another fact seized upon by future literary historians. Since there is no proof to the contrary, it is possible to picture young Will striking up an acquaintance with Michael Drayton at Polesworth Manor, or serving beer in Marianne Hacket's pub at Wincot, or living at Beauchamp Court as Fulke Greville's page, or acting as altarboy in a noble Catholic family, or butchering veal in the ancient style, as John Aubrey reports.

The truth of the matter is that the shadows enveloping these years do not disperse until the 27th and 28th of November, 1582, when we find an entry in the registry of the Bishop of Worcester recording that a marriage license was issued to William Shakespeare and Anne Hathaway. This entry is followed by an act in which two husbandmen of Stratford gave bonds of £40 'to defend and save harmless' the bishop and his officers should any legal obstacle to this marriage arise.

Six months later, on May 26, 1583, the Stratford priest baptized the first fruit of this hasty union, Susanna. Two years later, on February 2, 1585, he baptized Shakespeare's only other children, the twins Hamnet and Judith. In 1588 the name of Shakespeare appears again, this time in the records of a lawsuit brought against the poet's father by one of Mary Arden's nephews. And that is all we can glean from the official records concerning the poet's activities during this period. But at least

---

[1] In 1580 John Shakespeare was marked down as 'malecontent', bound over to keep the peace, and fined £40 for failure to appear at the Queen's bench.

we know that the 'provincial chapter' of his life was now drawing to a close, for when next we hear of him he was already in London, closely affiliated with the literary life and rowdy public of the Southwark theatres.

Although we can surmise that he left Stratford about 1587, the reasons that prompted him to leave remain shrouded in mystery. As usual there are several theories. The simplest – and most difficult to verify – has it that he left because of marital difficulties. To judge from his earliest comedies, Shakespeare did not at this time have a very exalted opinion of the institution of marriage. '*The venomous clamours of a jealous woman,*' he cries. '*Poison more deadly than a mad dog's tooth.*'[1] And again: '*I am asham'd that women are so simple to offer war where they should kneel for peace.*'[2] Should we agree with James Joyce, who seems convinced that Anne was the wooer, Will the wooed? 'He was chosen, it seems to me,' says Dedalus. 'If others have their will Ann hath a way. By cock, she was to blame. She put the comether on him, sweet and twenty-six. The grey-eyed goddess who bends over the boy Adonis, stooping to conquer, as prologue to the swelling act, is a boldfaced Stratford wench who tumbles in a cornfield a lover younger than herself.'[3] And, thinks Joyce, these memories were still with him when, in drawing up his will, Shakespeare left Anne his second best bed. Others doubt that Anne was the cause of the poet's departure for London: in 1690 the Reverend Richard Davies informed the world that Will had fled Stratford with the police on his heels for having poached at Charlecote in Thomas Lucy's park – Lucy being the 'consumptive magistrate' that Shakespeare later ridiculed as Justice Shallow:

> FALSTAFF. *Now, Master Shallow, you'll complain of me to the king?*
>
> SHALLOW. *Knight, you have beaten my men, killed my deer, and broke open my lodge.*
>
> FALSTAFF. *But not kissed your keeper's daughter?*[4]

The least imaginative of the critics say simply that the young man, having taught in a country school, was offered a better paying job in London. What sort of job? A keeper of horses for the theatregoers, say some; a notary's clerk, say others; while a

---

[1]   *The Comedy of Errors*, V, 1, 69–70.
[2]   *The Taming of the Shrew*, V, 2, 162–163.
[3]   James Joyce, *Ulysses*, p. 189. (Modern Library edition.)
[4]   *The Merry Wives of Windsor*, I, 1, 113–116.

third group assures us that he was a printer's helper. Less numerous are those who describe him as waging war in the Low Countries, fleeing the Catholic persecutions, or visiting those places in Italy and Navarre that he was soon to immortalize. But however tempting they may be, these legends are the halo around one irrefutable fact: by 1592 Shakespeare was in London, where he had already achieved a certain notoriety.

It was during the summer of 1592 that Robert Greene mentions Shakespeare in a pamphlet he wrote shortly before his death: *Greene's Groatsworth of Witte: bought with a Million of Repentaunce*. Reduced to utter poverty and mortally ill, the famous author of *Friar Bacon and Friar Bungay* bitterly deplored the ingratitude of those actors whose fame and fortune he had made. He wrote it as a farewell to his remaining friends to warn them lest the same fate befall them. 'Yes, trust them not,' he advised, adding that among these actors was 'an upstart crow, beautified with our feathers, that with his *Tygers heart wrapped in a Players hide*, supposes he is as well able to bumbast out a blanke verse as the best of you; and being an absolute *Johannes Factotum*, is in his owne conceit the only Shakes-scene in a countrie.' Although his name appears only as a pun, the reference throughout the passage is surely to Shakespeare. Moreover, the phrase about the 'tygers heart' is obviously a parody of the line:

'*Oh Tiger's heart wrapped in a woman's hide !*'

which appears both in *The True Tragedie of Richard Duke of Yorke*, and in the variant of that play which appears in the First Folio as the third part of *Henry VI*. At the time Greene wrote his pamphlet, the *Henry VI* series had just been staged so successfully that it doubtless had aroused both the admiration and jealousy of his rivals. But just how much of these plays is Shakespeare's own is again a matter of considerable controversy, and the critics are sharply divided concerning their authorship. Some scenes seem written in a pure Marlowe style, while the tone of others suggests the work of Greene. And, to add to the confusion, there are those who believe that Chapman wrote them. All of which would seem to justify the invective of the pamphleteer: a plagiarist, Shakespeare had apparently pilfered the texts of his contemporaries. Whatever the case may be, Greene, having vented his spite, died on September 3, 1592. Six months later Shakespeare made his official debut as an author with the publication of *Venus and Adonis*, which he dedicated to the Earl of Southampton.

44

VENVS
AND ADONIS

Vilia miretur vulgus: mihi flauus Apollo
Pocula Castalia plena ministret aqua.

LONDON

Imprinted by Richard Field, and are to be sold at
the signe of the white Greyhound in
Paules Church-yard.
1593.

At the time when the man from Stratford began his career as a poet, London already boasted three regular theatres. The first, simply called The Theatre, had been constructed in 1576 at Shoreditch, to the north of the city, by James Burbage, a member of Leicester's company. Shortly thereafter a second, The Curtain, was built close by. Then two others, the Newington Butts and the Rose, began drawing goodly crowds to the South bank of the Thames.

> *They say this town is full of cozenage;*
> *As, nimble jugglers that deceive the eye,*
> *Dark-working sorcerers that change the mind,*
> *Soul-killing witches that deform the body,*

Disguised cheaters, prating mountebanks,
And many such-like liberties of sin:
If it prove so, I will be gone the sooner.[1]

It would seem however that the actors failed to follow Antipholus' reasoning, since in 1592 the Swan opened its doors to the
public and in 1599 the Globe followed suit, both in this quarter
swarming with pickpockets and prostitutes. Year in and year
out, some fifty plays – from farce to tragedy – were performed
here to the delight of the crowds, which included both aristocrats

---

[1]   *The Comedy of Errors*, I, 2, 97–103.

and ne'er-do-wells. An intense rivalry grew up among the various acting groups, each of which enlivened its performances with jibes at its competitors:

> '*There is, sir, an aery of children, little eyases, that cry out on the top of question and are most tyranically clapp'd for't: these are now the fashion, and so berattle the common stages, – so they call them, – that many wearing rapiers are afraid of goose-quills, and dare scarce come hither.*'[1]

Most of the plays from these early years have disappeared, since they were never published. A few, such as Marlowe's *Tamburlaine*, Greene's *Friar Bacon*, and Kyd's *Spanish Tragedy* have come down to us. All we know about the others is that they contained a mixture of rowdy comedy and somber drama, and that the plot, between two or three murders, made liberal use of songs and poems.

> '*Here's one to a very doleful tune, how a userer's wife was brought to bed of twenty money-bags at a burden; and how she longed to eat adders' heads and toads carbonadoed... Here's another ballad of a fish that appeared upon the coast on Wednesday the fourscore of April, forty thousand fathoms above water, and sung this ballad against the hard hearts of maids...*'[2]

The scant evidence that has come down to us concerning these early plays seems ridiculously small in proportion to their number and quality. Three or four dissertations by Nashe, one of Philip Sydney's reviews, a moral diatribe by Stephen Gosson, a description of London by John Stow, a few *memoirs* from the pens of people who visited London, an essay by Thomas Dekker, some sermons by the Puritans, several official decrees – all of which are hardly sufficient to recreate the climate of this nascent art. Fortunately, starting in 1592, Henslowe's famous *Diary* helps fill in the gaps. Administrator of the Rose and the Swan, proprietor of the Fortune and the Hope, this power behind the English stage, whose step-daughter was to marry the famous actor Edward Alleyn, had begun keeping a record of the plays put on, expenses incurred for actors, manuscripts, costumes, and accessories.... Shakespeare's name does not appear in these records. 'Some

---

[1] *Hamlet*, II, 2, 362–368.
[2] *The Winter's Tale*, IV, 3, 264–267, 277–281.

people have found this astonishing,' notes Martin Maurice. 'But J. M. Robertson points out that the diary does not make mention of any payment made to any actor prior to 1597. And by that time Burbage's troupe – which had become the Lord Chamberlain's company – was no longer affiliated with Henslowe and no longer performed in any of his theatres. Since Shakespeare was a member of Burbage's company, this would explain the omission of his name from Henslowe's records.'[1]

What kind of life had the aspiring playwright been leading since his arrival in London? It is probable that he had been associating with the friends of a former classmate of his, Richard Field. By three years Shakespeare's elder, Field was the son of a Stratford tanner. This needy young man had found himself a job as clerk to Thomas Vautrollier, a French bookseller at Blackfriars. Eight years later, when his employer passed on to his reward, young Field came into possession of the printshop and, at the same time, of his late employer's wife. He was to distinguish himself at both these pursuits, of which the former has over the latter the advantage of having produced North's *Plutarch* and Ovid's *Metamorphoses*, two works that Shakespeare was to study and assimilate. For Shakespeare was already a frequent visitor at the shop if not, as certain wags imply, of the lady's bedchamber. 'Certain commentators have even suggested that, since she was French, Jacqueline Vautrollier – who in January of 1588 became 'Jacklin' Field – must have been dark and seductive, and that in trying to identify the dark enchantress who troubled the poet's peace of mind, she merits serious consideration, along with Mary Fitton, whose claims are dubious, and Mistress Davenport, who offers more serious references.'[2] But these frivolities are beside the point. What is important is that on April 18, 1593, Richard Field published a book entitled *Venus and Adonis* and had it registered at Stationer's Hall. It was signed by William Shakespeare and dedicated to Henry Wriothesley, the Earl of Southampton.

This classically handsome young nobleman, who had just taken his law degree at Cambridge, was extremely wealthy. It was probably during the presentation of *The Comedy of Errors* at Gray's Inn that Shakespeare insinuated himself into the Earl's good graces. Intelligent, cultured, a trifle vain, Southampton was soon to become the object of a veritable poetic cult. One after

[1] Martin Maurice, *Master William Shakespeare*, Gallimard, 1953, p. 60.
[2] Mrs. Longworth-Chambrun, *op. cit.*, p. 23.

49

the other Gervase Markham, Barnabe Barnes, and Samuel Daniel dedicated their verses to him. In one of his sonnets, Shakespeare voices his regret at this practice:

> *So oft have I invok'd thee for my Muse*
> *And found such fair assistance in my verse*
> *As every alien pen hath got my use*
> *And under thee their poesy disperse.* [1]

In 1593, however, Shakespeare was the high priest of this cult. The immediate success of *Venus and Adonis* apparently convinced him of the wisdom of his initial dedication, for the following year his friend Field published a second long poem, *The Rape of Lucrece*, which was preceded by an even warmer letter of dedication:

TO THE RIGHT HONOURABLE HENRY WRIOTHESLEY
EARL OF SOUTHAMPTON AND BARON OF TITCHFIELD

> *The love I dedicate to your lordship is without end; whereof this pamphlet, without beginning, is but a superfluous moiety. The warrant I have of your honourable disposition, not the worth of my untutored lines, makes it assured of acceptance. What I have done is yours; what I have to do is yours; being part in all I have, devoted yours. Were my worth greater, my duty would show greater; meantime, as it is, it is bound to your lordship, to which I wish long life, still lengthened with happiness.*

> *Your lordship's in all duty,*
> WILLIAM SHAKESPEARE

One can easily imagine that after such laudatory words as these, Southampton must have thrown open the doors of his estate to the poet. As chance would have it, one of these doors opened into the library, where Giovanni Florio was amassing a collection of Italian writers for the Earl. And it was doubtless thanks to the well-known grammarian that during these crucial years Shakespeare was able to come in contact with Ariosto, Boccaccio, Machiavelli, Bandello, Cinthio, Fiorentino and others, not to mention Rabelais, Montaigne and Belleforest. But Florio looked with a jaundiced eye at the imprudent pillaging of his books by this intruder. Prodded by Greene, in 1598 he accused him of being a carrion-crow who fed on others' riches.

---

[1] Sonnet LXXVIII.

TO THE RIGHT

HONOVRABLE, HENRY
VVriothesley, Earle of Southhampton,
and Baron of Titchfield.

THE loue I dedicate to your Lordship is without end: wherof this Pamphlet without beginning is but a superfluous Moity. The warrant I haue of your Honourable disposition, not the worth of my vntutord Lines makes it assured of acceptance. VVhat I haue done is yours, what I haue to doe is yours, being part in all I haue, deuoted yours. VVere my worth greater, my duety would shew greater, meane time, as it is, it is bound to your Lordship; To whom I wish long life still lengthned with all happinesse.

Your Lordships in all duety.

William Shakespeare.

A 2

And if he did? The cruelty of time is such that *Il Percorone*, the *Hecatommithi* and the *Novelle* have long since been forgotten, while *The Merchant of Venice*, *Othello* and *Romeo and Juliet* remain part of our immortal literary heritage. 'In matters of art,' said Wagner, who was speaking from experience, 'theft is justified only by assassination.'

If plagiarism was rife amongst the men of letters of the Elizabethan era, the plague was decimating the poorer quarters of the city. The Lord Mayor issued an order for the theatres to close their doors as soon as the weekly number of victims had reached a total of thirty. In fact, the same year which saw the publication of *Venus and Adonis* and *The Rape of Lucrece* was marked by a fresh outbreak of the plague. The various theatrical troupes were disbanded and did not return to London till the end of the summer of 1594. For a while Edward Alleyn nourished the hope of uniting

Edward Alleyn: a portrait of the actor.

both the Admiral's and Lord Chamberlain's companies into a single troupe and produced *The Taming of the Shrew* and *Titus Andronicus* at the Newington Butts. The attempt was short-lived however: in the autumn each company resumed its autonomy. Disheartened, Alleyn and his actors performed in Philip Henslowe's theatres, while the Burbages, Shakespeare and Kempe returned to the old Theatre at Shoreditch. From then on the two groups had very little contact with each another.

At the end of this same year, Shakespeare's name is mentioned for the first time in the accounts of the Treasurer of the Chamber. As a member of the Lord Chamberlain's company, he, along with Burbage and Kempe, was summoned during the Christmas season of 1594 to present some 'comedies and interludes' before the Queen at Greenwich Palace. Further evidence of Shakespeare's prominence in the theatre occurs in the famous passage of Francis Meres' *Palladis Tamia* (1598), in which the critic already names Shakespeare as the most important playwright in England: 'As Plautus and Seneca, among the Latins, are judged best for comedy and tragedy, so Shakespeare, among the English, is the most excellent in both kinds for the stage; for comedy, witness his Gentlemen of Verona, his Errors, his Love Labours Lost, his Love Labours Wonne, his Midsummers Night Dreame, and his Merchant of Venice; for tragedy, his Richard the 2, Richard the 3, Henry the 4, King John, Titus Andronicus, and his Romeo and Juliet.'

Shakespeare had already come a long way on the road from Stratford-on-Avon to celebrity. Two events, however, take us in 1596 back to the modest village of Warwickshire. On August 11th of that year Hamnet Shakespeare, the poet's only son, died at the age of 11. Though it appears doubtful that Shakespeare was ever very much of a father to his children, it is impossible to guess what repercussions such a misfortune might have had on his work and his soul. Certain critics see the initial causes of the poet's 'dark period' as stemming from Hamnet's death. Joyce, basing his theory on the troublesome analogy of names, even goes so far as to see in it one of the origins of *Hamlet*. Futile conjectures: the texts tell us nothing. Some have suggested that the deaths of Prince Arthur and of Mamillius, the young prince of Sicily, may have been based on the poet's own memories. Yet *King John* was written four years before Hamnet's death, and *The Winter's Tale* dates from 1611: if Shakespeare had really been deeply affected by the misfortune, it would indeed seem astonishing that he

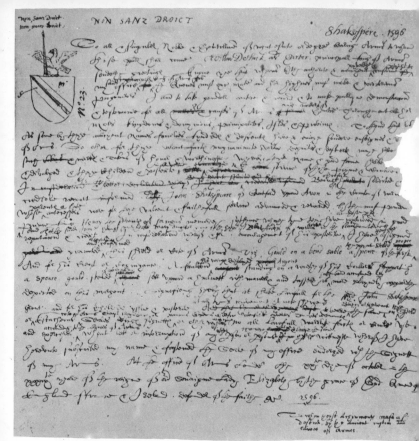

The license for Shakespeare's coat of arms.

waited fifteen years to express it. But what is not astonishing is that the critics have shown much less interest in the child's death than they have in the grant of arms that his grandfather applied for that same year from the College of Heralds. A draft granting that request was made up, but never executed. But in 1599 a renewed application was executed, giving the elder Shakespeare the right to bear the coat of arms described as follows: 'Gold, on a bend sable, a spear of the first, and for the crest or cognizance a falcon, his wings displayed argent, standing on a wreath of his colours, supporting a spear gold steeled aforesaid.' The motto is: 'Non sanz Droict.' Was it this honor that roused Ben Jonson's jealousy, causing him to jeer at Sogliardo's coat of arms and his motto: 'Non sans Moutarde'? The allusion at least leads us to believe that the theatre was acting as a good provider for the poet, and that in 'swelling his verse' Shakespeare also knew how to swell his purse.

'A poet,' said Greene, 'is a spendthrift and wastrel, born to make the tavern keepers rich and himself a beggar.' It is certain that Shakespeare could never have given such a detailed description of the dens and brothels where he led Falstaff unless he had personally spent some time in the Mermaid, the Boar's Head, the Mitre and the Dolphin. But in these bars, where Thomas Fuller pictured him as crossing verbal swords with Ben Jonson, he could not have squandered much of his fortune. That he was little given to prodigality is clearly evidenced by his indictment of Timon. And, says Joyce, 'He drew Shylock out of his own long pocket. The son of a maltjobber and money-lender he was himself a cornjobber and moneylender with ten tods of corn hoarded in the famine riots.'[1] The inventory of his acquisitions gives a good idea of his sense of property and economy. On May 4, 1597, he purchased from William Underwood, for *sexaginta libras sterlingorum*, the house to which he was later to retire: New Place, the largest house in Stratford. On the other hand, he was cited by the collectors of Saint Helen's parrish on November 15 as one of those whose taxes were in arrears. His name reappeared on this list during the next five years. On October 25, 1598, Richard Quiney, a Stratford draper, solicited (in vain, it appears) a loan of £30, and several letters exchanged between Quiney and a certain Abraham Sturley indicate that the poet was indeed doing very well for himself. On May 1, 1602, about 107 acres of arable land in Old Stratford were conveyed to the poet by William and John Combe, in consideration of £320; on September 28 of that same year, he purchased a cottage in Chapel Lane, Stratford. On July 24, 1605, Ralph Huband d'Ippesley surrendered to him, for £440, a part of the tithes of Stratford, Old Stratford, Welcombe and Bushopton. In 1607–8 he had a writ issued against a certain Addenbrooke who owed him £6. There are numerous other records and documents attesting to Shakespeare's purchases and financial transactions, but one final example shows that his investments were not

---

[1] James Joyce, *op. cit.*

confined to his native district. On March 10, 1613, he bought a house near the Blackfriars Theatre in London from Henry Walker. The price was £140, but the very next day Shakespeare

eGlobe

got Walker to mortgage the deed for £60, which he never seems to have repaid. One investment in particular has a direct bearing on his acting career. When James Burbage died in 1597, his sons

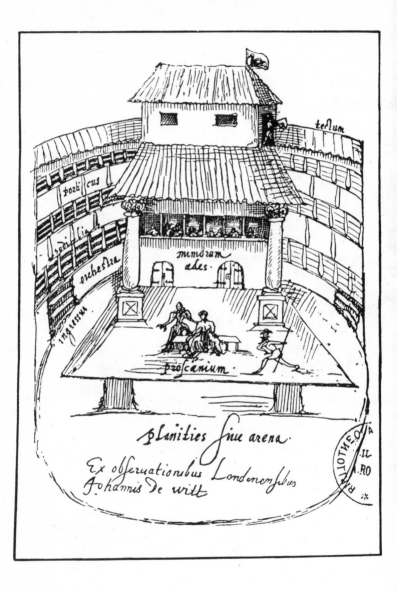

teſtum

porticus

ædificia

orcheſtra

mimorum
ædes

ingreſſus

proſcænium

planities ſiue arena.

Ex obſeruationibus Londinenſibus
Johannis de witt

Richard and Cuthbert had inherited the Theatre at Shoreditch. Their original lease had been granted in 1576, and when it expired the owner of the land on which the Theatre stood refused to renew it. After long negotiations, the company finally had to vacate the premises and cross the river to Southwark. There, near the Rose and the Swan, the Burbages erected a new theatre, the Globe. Keeping half the shares for themselves, they sold the rest to several members of their company, including Shakespeare, Heming, Condell and Philips. Thus did Shakespeare become a co-founder and co-owner of the most famous of the Elizabethan theatres. From then on he played almost exclusively at the Globe, except for his appearances at Court and at the dismantled monastery at Blackfriars, which the Burbages had leased when they were having difficulties with their lease for the Theatre.

We know from several descriptions, from a drawing by De Witt of the Swan, and from the construction contract for the Fortune Theatre, approximately what a public theatre looked like. The De Witt drawing is inaccurate in certain details, but it does give us a good general notion of the interior of the theatre. The public theatres were generally round – hexagonal or octagonal. In the center was the pit, where the people stood crowded together, eating, drinking, and jostling each other. Around the pit rose two or three tiers of galleries, covered by a thatched roof. Admission to the galleries sometimes cost as much as half a crown and was reserved for the wealthier patrons, while standing room in the pit could be had for as little as a penny. The stage, set about five feet above the level of the pit, was partly covered by a roof. Though it varied in size, it was generally about 25 feet wide and 30 feet deep. It projected about half way into the pit and was protected from it by a railing. This stage was divided into three parts: the outer stage, from which the pillars that supported the roof usually rose, was reserved for duels, battles, revels, and the like. Behind it was the inner stage, or alcove, which was separated from the outer stage by a curtain: it was here that deathbed and adultery scenes took place. Above the inner stage was a balcony, which could serve either as a maiden's bedchamber or castle ramparts. Depending on the circumstances, oriflammes, embroidered tapestries, or mourning cloth were hung from the balcony. From trapdoors cleverly built into the stage, ghosts and demons appeared; and the hut, or 'sky' – a room above the balcony – contained machinery for raising and lowering gods and 'dewey-eyed cherubs'. Aside from the tapestries, the scenery consisted only of the bare essentials: a tree was a forest, a rock a cliff, and to palliate the lack of imagination, a placard was often used to indicate the place of action. In sharp contrast to the barren stage, large sums of money were lavished on the costumes and disguises, and the use of velvet, brocade, satin, and lace was not uncommon. There were no women: women's roles were played by graceful young boys with high pitched voices. It is easy to see that the Elizabethan theatre demanded the whole-hearted complicity of the spectators:

Essex: a portrait of the condemned man.

> *But pardon, gentles all,*
> *The flat unraised spirits that hath dar'd*
> *On this unworthy scaffold to bring forth*
> *So great an object: can this cockpit hold*
> *The vasty fields of France? or may we cram*

> *Within this wooden O the very casques*
> *That did affright the air at Agincourt?*

and sought its encouragement:

> *Piece out our imperfections with your thoughts:*
> *Into a thousand parts divide one man,*
> *And make imaginary puissance;*
> *Think when we talk of horses that you see them*
> *Printing their proud hoofs i' the receiving earth;*
> *For 'tis your thoughts that now must deck our kings,*
> *Carry them here and there, jumping o'er times,*
> *Turning the accomplishment of many years*
> *Into an hour-glass.'* [1]

It is doubtless because of the strong hold the theatre had on the public that Essex and his accomplices decided to use it as an instrument of political propaganda. The causes of the abortive rebellion are well known. Essex's fiery character, his military defeats, his outbursts in Parliament, his extravagant debts, all had hastened the day of his disgrace. Since the inglorious and unexpected return of the hero, whom Shakespeare had pictured as returning from Ireland 'with the revolt impaled upon his sword', Cecil's faction had turned the Queen irrevocably against him. Having seen every honor he sought – from Secretary of State to a monopoly of the wine trade – stubbornly refused him, the enraged Essex secretly sounded out James VI, either with a view to actually deposing the Queen or at least imposing his demands upon her. On February 6, 1601, his accomplices visited the Globe and asked the directors, in return for a payment of 40 shillings, to stage *Richard II*. Were they referring to Shakespeare's *Richard II*? More than one critic today claims they were not, noting that this play seems more a defense of the legitimate sovereign than an incitement to rebellion. But it is hard to believe that the Globe had several similar tragedies, and it is highly possible that for this occasion Shakespeare toned down the passages stigmatizing Bolingbroke's crime. Revised or not, the play was performed on February 7th. On the 8th the revolt failed miserably. On the 25th Essex was beheaded, and his lieutenant, Southampton, had his sentence commuted to life imprisonment. The quasi-complicity of

---

[1] *Henry V*, Prologue, 8–14, 23–31.

the Lord Chamberlain's company did not prevent them from performing at court that same week.

Meanwhile, Shakespeare went on with his work. In 1598 Andrew Wise had printed the first part of *King Henry IV;* that same year Cuthbert Burbage entered at Stationer's Hall: *The most excellent Historie of the Merchant of Venice. With the extreame crueltye of Shylocke the Iewe towards the sayd Merchant, in cutting a iust pound of his flesh: and the obtayning of Portia by the choyse of three chests. As it has often been represented by the Servants of the Lord Chamberlain. Written by William Shakespeare.* In 1600 the following plays were inscribed in this official Register where the censors recorded the permissions to print that had been granted: *Henry IV, Part II; Much Ado About Nothing; A Midsummer Night's Dream....* But little by little a strange melancholy began to pervade the poet's characters. The sentiments he had formerly extolled seemed empty and false to him:

> *Thou common friend, that's without faith or love,*
> *For such is a friend now!*[1]

His most exquisite comedies were already ending on a note of profound bitterness:

> *Blow, blow, thou winter wind,*
> *Thou art not so unkind*
> *As man's ingratitude.*

The vanity of those in power, the folly of lovers, the treachery of friends: as if he were ridding himself of some long-held illusions, Shakespeare at last entered the truth of tragedy.

More than one exegete has thought that the key to this evolution was to be found in the *Sonnets.* But this assertion seems especially dubious, since we know nothing at all about their composition. Published in 1609 by Thomas Thorpe – without the author's assent, it seems – at least a portion of the sonnets had appeared by 1598, since Francis Meres mentions them in his *Palladis Tamia.* But no other existing document gives us the slightest clue as to their origin. It is even questionable whether Shakespeare ever intended them for publication. There are numerous indications that he did not, of which the most obvious is the equivocal, even

---

[1]   *The Two Gentlemen of Verona*, V, 4, 62–63.

SHAKE-SPEARES

SONNETS.

Neuer before Imprinted.

AT LONDON
By *G. Eld* for *T. T.* and are
to be folde by *Iohn Wright,* dwelling
at Chrift Church gate.
1609.

WHen in the Chronicle of wasted time,
    I see discriptions of the fairest wights,
And beautie making beautifull old rime,
In praise of Ladies dead, and louely Knights,
Then in the blazon of sweet beauties best,
Of hand, of foote, of lip, of eye, of brow,
I see their antique Pen would haue exprest,
Euen such a beauty as you maister now.
So all their praises are but prophesies
Of this our time, all you prefiguring,
And for they look'd but with deuining eyes,
They had not still enough your worth to sing:
    For we which now behold these present dayes,
    Haue eyes to wonder, but lack toungs to praise.

107

NOt mine owne feares, nor the prophetick soule,
    Of the wide world, dreaming on things to come,
Can yet the lease of my true loue controule,
Supposde as forfeit to a confin'd doome.
The mortall Moone hath her eclipse indur'de,
And the sad Augurs mock their owne presage,
Incertenties now crowne them-selues assur'de,
And peace proclaimes Oliues of endlesse age.
Now with the drops of this most balmie time,
My loue lookes fresh, and death to me subscribes,
Since spight of him Ile liue in this poore rime,
While he insults ore dull and speachlesse tribes.
    And thou in this shalt finde thy monument,
    When tyrants crests and tombs of brasse are spent.

108

WHat's in the braine that Inck may character,
    Which hath not figur'd to thee my true spirit,
What's new to speake, what now to register,
That may expresse my loue, or thy deare merit?
Nothing sweet boy, but yet like prayers diuine,

I must

scandalous nature of the experience described. In fact, 'this belated and neglected edition, with its mysterious, abnormal and obscure dedication, would not only seem to be a pirated edition, but a publication actually instigated by a rival clique whose aim was to defame Shakespeare and his followers, and perhaps more specifically to cast aspersions on the most influential member of his circle, the poet's protector'.[1] Even assuming that Shakespeare approved of their publication, in what order did he want them presented? Countless researchers have studied every rhyme, every period and comma in an effort to discover, as with Pascal's *Pensées*, the logical order of their inspiration. But what does logic matter here? And, lacking a better classification, why not keep to the one offered by Thorpe? Everything about the sonnets – not only why they were written but how they were written – remains an enigma.

Preceded by a dedication to the mysterious W. H., the *Sonnets* are divided into two sections which are separated by a twelve-line poem. The first 125 deal with a blond young man, the last 28 with a dark young lady. These two main sections can be further broken down into several smaller sub-divisions, each with a dominant theme:

I. *The lover's cycle* (1–126)

1–17: the poet urges a friend, whom he describes as young, handsome, and of high station, to beget a son in his own image.

18–26: he assures this friend of a devotion that he hopes will be immortalized by his verse and, to make sure there is no mis-understanding, specifies:

> *A woman's face with Nature's own hand painted*
> *Hast thou, the master-mistress of my passion.*

27–33: now this passion turns to sorrow; the poet complains of his solitude and abandonment, though he still experiences some happy moments in knowing he is loved.

34–42: his friend has cruelly betrayed him by seducing his mistress; deceived, he is upset about it; generous, he forgives; obliging, he approves; an accomplice, he says, '*Take all my loves, my love, yea, take them all.*'

---

[1] Charles-Marie Garnier, Introduction to the *Sonnets*, Les Belles Lettres, p. ix.

43–53: separated from his beloved, no doubt by a voyage, the poet alternates between moments of melancholy and explosions of joy.

54–70: meditations on time, change, death.

71–77: the poet calls for death, oblivion, but, being past all sense of shame, comes back to his love:

> *Oh know, sweet love, I always write of you,*
> *And you and love are still my argument.*

78–87: a rival poet has usurped his place, whence jealousy, sacrifice, farewells.

88–108: back from his voyage, the victim harks back to his grievances, his lamentations, his oaths.

109–119: the poet in turn confesses his infidelity, implores indulgence, and convinces himself that his sincerity will atone for it.

120–125: all is forgiven; doubts and afflictions give way to serenity.

126: an invocation to Time.

II. *The mistress' cycle* (127–154)

127–143: decidedly eclectic, the poet declares his love for a dark lady, then, almost in the same breath, accuses her of being false, lewd and of having debauched his young friend.

144–152: the lovers are far apart now; and will he, the forsaken lover, continue to languish with desire? no, for he is more faithless than she:

> *But why of two oaths' breach do I accuse thee*
> *When I break twenty?*

He forgives her and resolves to keep her, so that everyone may be happy.

153–154: two epigrams to Cupid confirm this happy end.

We can see the riddles that this most edifying story poses. For one thing, who is W. H.? Are W. H. and the blond young man of the sonnets the same person? Who is the dark lady? And who is the rival poet? It goes without saying that here, as elsewhere, the critics are far from being unanimous in their opinions. Though there is fairly general agreement that W. H. is indeed the young man to whom the poet speaks in the first section of the sonnets, when it comes to naming him there are almost as many candidates as there are critics. The most plausible hypothesis is that W. H. was Henry Wriothesley, whose initials were inverted by the publisher as a measure of discretion, precaution, or as a prank. Tyler and Chambers, on the other hand, believe that W. H. was William Herbert, the Earl of Pembroke, to whom Heminge and Condell dedicated the Folio of 1623, in recognition of the services he had rendered Shakespeare. Others, harking back to the poet's family, see the initials as referring to either of the poet's brothers-in-law, William Hart or William Hathaway. Still others maintain that the initials refer to the unlicensed broker William Hall, the person who apparently secured the manuscript of sonnets for Thomas Thorpe. More recently, Oscar Wilde, by an easily understandable deformation, conjured up the existence of a William Hews, a young actor of the Shakespearean troupe, whom the poet... but let's not go into details.

The candidates for the title of Shakespeare's 'dark lady' are equally numerous. Southampton's followers suspect that Mistress Davenant, an Oxford innkeeper, may well have carried her hospitality as far as the bedchamber whenever her friends were passing through. Pembroke's partisans cast their vote for Mary Fitton, one of the Queen's ladies-in-waiting and Pembroke's mistress: unfortunately for their cause, however, two portraits of the lady discovered in 1897 reveal that her hair was light brown. Not that that would stop them! Jacqueline Vautrollier and Penelope Devereux, Essex's sister, are also on the list, which also latterly includes a dusky courtesan named Lucy Negro.

James I: the picture of indulgence.

As for the rival poet, it may have been Barnabe Barnes or Samuel Daniel, depending on whether one subscribes to the Wriothesley or Herbert theory. But neither Spenser, Marlowe, Jonson, Marston, Nashe, Markham or Drayton are excluded as possibilities, while the name of Chapman occurs more frequently than all the rest.

But after exploring all these intriguing possibilities, one is confronted by another, even more intriguing enigma: did Shakespeare really experience what he relates in his sonnets, or did he purely and simply make them up? It is common knowledge that all poetry does not necessarily proceed from actual experience, and the sonnets contain a sufficient number of generalities to suggest the possibility that they were the product of his imagination. Thus there are two schools of thought: the 'personal', originating with Malone and Wordsworth, which considers these poems as autobiographical, and the 'impersonal', championed by Keats and Browning, which takes them to be mere creations of the mind. But it seems obvious that the *Sonnets*, whether subjective or objective, do express a crisis, and that certain passages at least prove it was a very real crisis in the poet's life:

> *Two loves I have of comfort and despair,*
> *Which like two spirits do suggest me still:*
> *The better angel is a man right fair,*
> *The worser spirit a woman, colour'd ill.*

This possible crisis was compounded in 1601 by two other strokes of misfortune: the imprisonment of the poet's benefactor and the death of his father. The shadow of death has already infiltrated his work, tempering his lyricism and making his world one in which the powers of evil are extolled. In this same fateful year, *Julius Caesar* inaugurates a whole series of plays whose source of inspiration seems to be the universe itself.

Following the execution of Essex, however, the long reign of Elizabeth entered its final phase. On March 25, 1603, the news was finally voiced throughout the kingdom that the Queen was dead at Richmond and that James VI of Scotland had, by divine right, succeeded to the throne as James I of England. It is a well-known fact that during the period of public mourning that followed the Queen's death, Shakespeare was especially conspicuous by his silence. We can only guess whether this silence stemmed from his resentment as a Catholic, an innate disdain for public manifestations of this sort, or from a basic lack of conformity. It was

The Workes of William Shakefpeare,

containing all his Comedies, Hiftories, and
Tragedies: Truely fet forth, according to their firft
ORIGINALL.

The Names of the Principall Actors
in all thefe Playes.

Illiam Shakefpeare.

Richard Burbadge.

John Hemmings.

Augufline Phillips.

William Kempt.

Thomas Poope.

George Bryan.

Henry Condell.

William Slye.

Richard Cowly.

John Lowine.

Samuell Croffe.

Alexander Cooke.

Samuel Gilburne.

Robert Armin.

William Oftler.

Nathan Field.

John Underwood.

Nicholas Tooley.

William Ecclefrone.

Jofeph Taylor.

Robert Benfield.

Robert Goughe.

Richard Robinfon.

Iohn Shancke.

Iohn Rice.

THE

Tragicall Hiſtorie of

HAMLET

Prince of Denmarke

By William Shake-ſpeare.

As it hath beene diuerſe times acted by his Highneſſe ſer-
uants in the Cittie of London : as alſo in the two V-
niuerſities of Cambridge and Oxford, and elſe-where

At London printed for N.L. and Iohn Trundell.
1603.

The first Hamlet.

not until ten years later that he atoned for it in a series of pompous
verses in *Henry VIII* meant to flatter the new king:

> But as when
> The bird of wonder dies, the maiden phoenix,
> Her ashes new-create another heir
> As great in admiration as herself,
> So shall she leave her blessedness to one, –
> When heaven shall call her from this cloud of darkness, –
> Who from the sacred ashes of her honour,
> Shall star-like rise . . .

70

Wherever the bright sun of heaven shall shine,
His honour and the greatness of his name
Shall be, and make new nations.[1]

Although he never quite succeeded in fulfilling these laudatory prophecies, James I at least inaugurated his reign with a liberal display of clemency. One of his initial acts was to free Southampton, restoring to him not only his confiscated possessions, but also granting him an additional 6000 crowns. Freed from the Tower on April 10, 1603, the Earl was ceremoniously received by the king, who showered him with numerous honors and enjoined him to take his place at the head of his retinue. This homage, publicly paid to one of Elizabeth's avowed enemies, gave a good indication of the course the new regime intended to pursue. All those who by confession, opinion, affiliations, or activities had suffered during the preceding reign were ostentatiously restored to their former positions. And among the first to be so honored were the members of the Lord Chamberlain's company, whom 'good Queen Bess' had never understood or helped, and who now were appointed the King's men. A royal Patent of May 17 and May 19, 1603, authorized 'Lawrence Fletcher, William Shakespeare, Richard Burbage, Augustine Phillips, John Heminge, Henry Condell, William Sly, Robert Armin, Richard Cowley, and the rest of their associates freely to use and exercise the art of playing comedies, tragedies, histories, interludes, morals, pastorals, stage-plays... for the recreation of our loving subjects as for our solace and pleasure when we shall think good to see them.' The patent also stated that they could perform not only 'within their now usual house called The Globe', plague permitting, but also 'within any town-halls or other convenient places in any city, university, town or borough whatsoever', and all Justices, Mayors, Sheriffs, Constables, Headboroughs and other officers were commanded to 'aid and assist them'. When we recall the £20 that had been allocated to them in 1594 to perform several comedies and interludes before the Queen, and noting that they were paid £80 for their Christmas performance in 1604, we can see that their promotion was more than a merely honorary one. Thus freed from material worries, the tyranny of the censors and the demands of the public, the poet's genius was able to blossom forth unhindered.

---

[1] *Henry VIII*, V, 5, 40–53.

An initial – and defective – edition of *Hamlet* had appeared in 1603. The publication in 1604 of the definitive version of this play marks one of the high points of the Shakespearean career. In this same year, *Measure For Measure* extolled, in the person of the Duke of Vienna, the justice and clemency of James I, while *All's Well that Ends Well*, *Othello*, and *The Merry Wives of Windsor* fully established the fame of the dramatist. Meanwhile, his fame as an actor was also growing. On December 26th the new company put on *The Comedy of Errors* at the Court; in January, 1605, *Love's Labour's Lost* and *Henry V*. On February 10th their performance of *The Merchant of Venice* so pleased the king that he ordered it played again on the 12th. But, by its allusions to Scottish history, to the ascendency of James I and to his penchant for occultism and sorcery, as well as by its brilliant lyricism and philosophy, no triumph of these fertile years can compare with *Macbeth*. Henceforth anything seemed possible to this poet who was the first since Aeschylus to give tragedy universal dimensions. In 1607 Shakespeare crowned this uninterrupted effort with the most impressive, the most extraordinary of his creations: *King Lear*.

The royal company, acclaimed by the public for its triumphs at the Globe, applauded by the nobility for its performances at Whitehall and Hampton Court, was in 1608 to enlarge still further its sphere of activities. The elder Burbage, an indefatigable prospector, had acquired another theatre in his declining days: the indoor theatre which he had converted from the dismantled convent at Blackfriars. Famous for its comfort and luxury, this new acquisition was also noteworthy as London's first covered theatre. Its clientele was restricted to the wealthier patrons of the theatre, the same public that Shakespeare contrasted with the boorish public of the pits in *Hamlet*. When their father died, Richard and Cuthbert Burbage rented Blackfriars to Henry Evans and his children's company. These 'little falcons' were not deterred by their youth from engaging in the freest sort of repartee, a custom which doubly infuriated the Puritan members of the Council. Not content with having poked fun at the king's accent in *Eastward Ho!* these youngsters staged one of Chapman's satires which ridiculed both Henry IV and his mistress. After the French ambassador lodged an official protest, the play was proscribed. But shortly thereafter, since the Court had just left London, the children put it on again. This time the troupe was irrevocably dissolved, and Evans was forced to return the theatre to its owners. On August 9th the Burbages, Shakespeare, Heminge, Condell, and Sly divided the shares among them and became co-owners of the Blackfriars. From then on they alternated between the Globe and the Blackfriars, playing at the former during the summer and at the latter during the winter season. It was probably in this former convent that those plays which, to use Farnham's expression, mark 'the tragic frontier of the Shakespearean theater,' were first presented: *Timon of Athens, Anthony and Cleopatra, Coriolanus....*

And yet the poet, tired of the city, was more and more obsessed by the thought of withdrawing from it, as his works of this period

New Place.

will testify. On June 5, 1607, he returned to Stratford for the marriage of his daughter Susanna to Dr. John Hall. He was then at the height of his fame. It is also possible that the death of his mother two years later suddenly intensified his weariness. But we are no more certain of the exact date he left the stage than we are of when he started his theatrical career. From 1610 on, however, he seems to have divided his time more and more between the London theatres and his Stratford residence, New Place. By 1611 the rupture was almost complete. Shakespeare entrusted the responsibilities for his theatrical interests to his associates and returned to the scenes of his early life to write the three masterpieces of serenity: *Cymbeline*, *The Winter's Tale*, and *The Tempest*.

> *Being so reputed*
> *In dignity, and for the liberal arts,*
> *Without a parallel: those being all my study,*
> *The government I cast upon my brother,*
> *And to my state grew stranger, being transported*
> *And rapt in secret studies.*[1]

This solitude was interrupted only by rare visits to the capital. On May 11, 1612, he appeared there as a witness in a trial between his former landlord, Christopher Mountjoy, in whose house he had apparently lived from 1598 to 1604, and Mountjoy's son-in-law, Stephen Bellott. On March 10, 1613, Shakespeare, together with William Johnson, the lessee of the Mermaid tavern, John Jackson, and John Heminge, purchased that curious house in the Blackfriars district which served as a haunt for Catholic recusants. On March 31st of the same year he received the sum of 44 shillings for having constructed and painted a heraldic device for the Earl of Rutland, who had used it in a tournament at Whitehall the week before.[2] On July 2nd, the Globe was destroyed by a fire that began during a performance of *Henry VII*, thus bringing to a symbolic end the career of the greatest playwright of the age.

The poet's last years were spent amidst the peace and beauty of the country. His work completed, it would seem that Shakespeare, like his father before him, took an active part in municipal affairs, and was involved in the dispute over the proposed enclosure of certain common fields that belonged to the town of Stratford. On February 10, 1616, he was present at the marriage

---

[1] *The Tempest.* I, 2, 72–77.
[2] Burbage's skill as a painter is well known, and it was probably he who executed the design, while Shakespeare supplied the motto.

of his daughter Judith to the son of that same Richard Quiney, who, almost twenty years before, had tried to borrow £30 from him. On March 25th, feeling his death at hand he drew up his will before witnesses:

In the name of God, Amen! I William Shackspeare, of Stratford upon Avon in the countie of Warr., gent., in perfect health and memorie, God be praysed, doe make and ordayne this my last will and testament in manner and forme followeing, that ys to saye. ffirst, I commend my soule into the handes of God my Creator, hoping and assuredlie beleeving, through

Dr. Hall's office.

*the onlie merittes, of Jesus Christe my Saviour, to be made
partaker of lyfe everlastinge, and my bodye to the earth
whereof yt ys made.*

Item, he named John Hall and Susanna his legal heirs and
executors of his estate; he bequeathed, under certain conditions,
£150 to his daughter Judith, and gave his silverware and various
other objects and possessions to his sister, his nephews, his grand-
daughter, his goddaughter, his friends and neighbors; he bequeathed 28s. 8d. to his colleagues Burbage, Heminge, and
Condell '*to buy them ringes*'. And to his wife Anne, '*I gyve my
second best bed with the furniture*', a gift of less value, certainly,
than the '*tenn pounds*' he willed to '*the poore of Stratford*'.
Thus at peace with his family and friends, Shakespeare was ready
to pass into that other world where he had already dispatched so
many of his heroes. Legend has it that in April Ben Jonson, by
a final act of treachery, paid the poet a visit in company with
Michael Drayton and got Shakespeare to quaff so many tankards
that he was bloated from it. Dr. Hall, the poet's son-in-law,
managed to save Drayton *in extremis* by the administration of a
certain elixir of violets. Could this imply that, anxious to profit
from Shakespeare's recently drafted will, he deprived his father-
in-law of the healing virtues of this panacea? Might not those
three prophetic lines from *Julius Caesar* have flashed through the
dying poet's mind:

> *This day I breathed first; time is come round,*
> *And where I did begin, there shall I end;*
> *My life is run his compass.*[1]

---

[1] *Julius Caesar*, V, 3, 23–25.

The choir and the tomb.

GOOD FREND FOR IESVS SAKE FORBEARE,
TO DIGG THE DVST ENCLOASED HEARE.
BLESE BE Y MAN y SPARES THES STONES
AND CVRST BE HE Y MOVES MY BONES

Like Cassius, who died on his birthday, the man who so often had written of death and resurrection died on April 23, 1616. He was buried in Trinity Church, Stratford, on the 25th. If he died a 'papist' we have no evidence of it. On his gravestone were inscribed the four simple lines of verse which can still be seen there today:

> Good friend, for Jesus' in sake forebeare
> To digg the dust encloased heare;
> Bleste be the man that spares these stones,
> And curst be he that moves my bones.

A portrait of Burbage.

Now does my project gather to a head: My charms crack not; my spirits obey, and time Goes upright with his carriage.

The Tempest

The Works and Days

Books whose dates of composition are clearly established tell their own story. From one to the other we can follow the progress of the problems, ideas, and images that relate more or less directly to the author's life. We learn that a certain reflection preceded a certain theme, that this denial followed that affirmation; in short, we can reconstruct in time what time itself tends to fuse together: the complexity of the mind. Not so with Shakespeare. The tremendous difficulty that anyone who tries to penetrate his universe encounters is no doubt caused by a lack of detailed knowledge concerning its parts. We scarcely know how to classify his disconcerting plays, and the critics who have tried to do so have had to depend, aside from their personal preferences or prejudices, on data and documents that are extremely suspect.

There are however a few well established facts: at the time of the poet's death, aside from *Venus and Adonis*, *The Rape of Lucrece*, *The Passionate Pilgrim*, *The Phoenix and the Turtle*, and the *Sonnets*, some twenty plays had appeared either under his signature or his initials,[1] of which thirteen are still attributed to

---

[1] There are, of course, some thirty-seven plays generally attributed to Shakespeare: the thirty-six of the First Folio plus *Pericles*. But at the time of the poet's death only twenty plays had appeared either under his name or his initials. As noted, seven of these are today rejected as spurious; that they were published as Shakespeare's is a good indication of his high esteem, for by so signing them their authors were attempting to profit from the Shakespeare name.

him: *Love's Labour's Lost*, *Richard III*, *Richard II*, the first and second parts of *Henry IV*, *The Merchant of Venice*, *Much Ado About Nothing*, *A Midsummer Night's Dream*, *The Merry Wives of Windsor*, *Hamlet*, *King Lear*, *Troilus and Cressida* and *Pericles*. The other seven, generally rejected as spurious, are: *The Tragedy of Locrine*, *Sir John Oldcastle*, *The History of Thomas Lord Cromwell*, *The London Prodigal*, *The Puritan Widow*, *A Yorkshire Tragedy*, and *The Troublesome Reign of King John*. Among the plays enumerated by Francis Meres in 1598, neither *The Two Gentlemen of Verona* nor *The Comedy of Errors* was printed. And what about the mysterious *Love's Labours Wonne*? On the other hand, *Titus Andronicus*, *Romeo and Juliet*, *The Taming of the Shrew*, *Henry V*, and two earlier plays corresponding to the second and third parts of *Henry VI*: *The Entire Battle Between the two Famous Houses of York and Lancaster* and *The True Tragedy of Richard Duke of York* had been published anonymously. Of the plays written in collaboration with Fletcher, one of them, *Cardenio*, has disappeared, while the other, *The Two Noble Kinsmen*, has today been rejected as part of the Shakespeare apocrypha.

The care of publishing Shakespeare's collected works logically befell the faithful Burbage. But when Burbage died in 1619, two other Globe actors, John Heminge and Henry Condell, assumed the responsibility. Weeding out the fraudulent quartos, gathering together all the authentic texts, they managed with a great deal of difficulty to publish the monumental First Folio in 1623. Prefaced by Droeshout's portrait of Shakespeare and Ben Jonson's ten-line stanza, dedicated to the Earls of Pembroke and Montgomery, it also contained an 'Address to the Readers' by Heminge and Condell, and eulogizing poems by Hugh Holland, Leonard Digges and James Mabbe, as well as Ben Jonson's famous ode. The First Folio contained thirty-six of Shakespeare's plays, omitting only *Pericles, Prince of Tyre*, and classified them into three groups: comedies, histories, and tragedies. By adopting this classification, Heminge and Condell unfortunately, though deliberately, sacrificed chronological order for logical order. Henceforth the problem of determining the chronology of Shakespeare's creations added one more enigma to the count of the poet whom Ernest Jones has rightly called 'the Sphinx of modern literature'.

There is indeed no work in the entire history of our culture in which logic and chronology make such poor bedfellows. The

A CATALOGVE

of the seuerall Comedies, Histories, and Tragedies contained in this Volume.

most important reason for this of course is the fact that in Shakespeare's time playwrights were less concerned about being read than being played. Often many years elapsed before a play which had been mentioned by the chroniclers of the time, seen by the public, and applauded or hooted, was honored by publication. In the interim countless plagiarists had ample opportunity to pilfer it, till the day when the author himself came forward to claim it as his own. All these difficulties explain the contradictions with which modern critics have continually to contend. Take *Titus Andronicus*, for example: mentioned the 24th of January, 1594, in Henslowe's diary, recorded the 6th of February in Stationer's Register, this play must have been written, according to all evidence, by 1593. But this raises an initial question: was this *Titus* really Shakespeare's, or was it perhaps an earlier version he drew upon to write the play mentioned by Francis Meres? And this mystery is complicated by a second: if Shakespeare is really the author of this play, then it must represent one of his earliest efforts; and yet it contains many analogies to his later tragedies.

Titus Andronicus has often been classified as one of the first plays of Elizabethan drama. In a sense, its atmosphere recalls that of Kyd's *Spanish Tragedy;* its theme, revenge, Marlowe's *Jew of Malta;* and the villain, Aaron, closely resembles Barrabas. It would therefore seem that this melodrama was indeed one of Shakespeare's earliest plays, an adaptation of works by Kyd and Marlowe. Further proof can be found in eight lines of an anonymous comedy, *A Knack to Know a Knave*, which was first performed on June 10, 1592: these lines unquestionably refer to Titus, conquerer of the Goths. This would place the composition of Shakespeare's *Titus* as early as 1590–91. At that time he was unknown, and if we accept this date as being correct, why did Henslowe speak of it as being performed for the first time only three years later?

And what is more, this tragedy, in spite of all the proofs to the contrary, seems less a product of Shakespeare's youth than of his maturity. It is difficult to believe that its style is contemporary to *The Two Gentlemen of Verona* or to the euphuisms of *Love's Labour's Lost*. The impassioned imagery, improbable plot and the succession of murders and atrocities it contains evoke Webster, Ford, and Tourneur more than Kyd or Marlowe. As for the characters themselves, they are closely related to those Shakespeare created between 1604 and 1610. For cruelty, hypocrisy, and ambition, Tamora, Queen of the Goths, has only one equal: Lady

Macbeth. In the odious person of Aaron, her lover, we find a sort of synthesis of Othello and his demon, Iago. And if there is one hero whom Titus Andronicus heralds, it is assuredly King Lear. Besides which, the corruption of Rome is stigmatized in terms which portend *Timon of Athens*. The general who, enraged by his country's infamy, defects to the enemy and marches against the ungrateful city, really belongs to the plot of *Coriolanus*. Finally, the story of the abandoned child who is secretly taken to a barbarian land to escape persecution, forms an important episode of *The Winter's Tale;* the same occurs in *Titus Andronicus* when Aaron, having had an illegitimate son by Tamora, prepares to save him from the wrath of the Romans.

Thus we have an example of a play which dates unquestionably from Shakespeare's youth and yet, for numerous reasons, seems definitely to belong to his 'dark period'. This gives some idea of the difficulties in store for anyone attempting a strict classification of the plays. Depending on whether one accepts such and such a document as authentic or spurious, the classification changes completely; and depending on whether a given drama precedes or follows a given comedy, the meaning of the order is changed. Similar complications justify the increasing importance of historical and textual commentaries. But since the specialists are far from agreeing on the matter, we could not do better than to list the following chronologies established by two of the most eminent Shakespearean scholars, G. B. Harrison and G. L. Kittredge:

HARRISON		KITTREDGE	
1591.	Henry VI, part I	1590–91.	Henry VI, part II
	Henry VI, part II	1591.	Henry VI, part III
	Henry VI, part III	1591–92.	Henry VI, part I
1591.	Richard III	1592.	Richard III
	Titus Andronicus	1592–93.	The Comedy of Errors
	Love's Labour's Lost	1593.	Titus Andronicus
	The Two Gentlemen of Verona	1594.	The Two Gentlemen of Verona
	The Comedy of Errors		King John
	The Taming of the Shrew	1594–95.	Love's Labour's Lost
1594.	Romeo and Juliet	1594–98.	The Taming of the Shrew
	A Midsummer Night's Dream	1595.	Romeo and Juliet
	Richard II		A Midsummer Night's Dream
	King John	1596.	The Merchant of Venice
	The Merchant of Venice		Richard II
1597.	Henry IV, part I	1597.	Henry IV, part I
	Henry IV, part II		Henry IV, part II

83

	Left list		Right list
	Much Ado About Nothing	1598–99.	Much Ado About Nothing
	The Merry Wives of Windsor		
	As You Like It	1599.	As You Like It
	Julius Caesar		Henry V
	Henry V		Julius Caesar
	Troilus and Cressida	1600–1.	The Merry Wives of Windsor
1601.	Hamlet		
	Twelfth Night		Twelfth Night
	Measure for Measure		Hamlet
	All's Well that Ends Well	1602	All's Well that Ends Well
	Othello		Troilus and Cressida
1606.	King Lear	1604.	Othello
	Macbeth		Measure for Measure
	Timon of Athens	1605–6.	Macbeth
	Anthony and Cleopatra		King Lear
	Coriolanus	1605–8.	Timon of Athens
1609.	Pericles, Prince of Tyre	1606–8.	Pericles, Prince of Tyre
1611.	Cymbeline	1607.	Anthony and Cleopatra
1611.	The Winter's Tale	1608.	Coriolanus
	The Tempest	1610.	Cymbeline
	Henry VIII	1610–11.	The Tempest
		1611.	The Winter's Tale
		1613.	Henry VIII

A cursory examination of these lists, though it reminds us that appreciable differences do exist among scholars concerning the dating of Shakespeare's plays, should also convince us of the necessity for rejecting any schematic concept of this theatre. Of course it would be convenient to adopt, as many others have done, the order perpetuated in the textbooks: comedies, histories, and tragedies. While such a classification would not provide us with a true picture of the situation, it would at least simplify matters greatly. Its very coherence appeals to our common sense, much as do truisms such as the oft repeated, 'Racine portrays men as they are; Corneille as they should be', etc. What could be more obvious? A talented young man begins by trying his hand at comedy; having achieved a certain mastery of his art, he ventures into the more exacting realm of historical drama and finally, daring to believe in his own genius, creates the masterful tragedies of the later period... Such an orderly evolution is, unhappily, in flagrant contradiction with the facts. Far from confirming it, any comparison of various chronologies shows us that, on the contrary, Shakespeare was working simultaneously in all three dramatic forms. It even appears that the outset of his career was characterized rather by *Richard III*, *Titus Andronicus*, and *King John* than by *The Comedy of Errors* or *The Two Gentlemen of Verona*.

Between such entertaining comedies as *The Taming of the Shrew* and *A Midsummer Night's Dream* is placed the tragic legend of *Romeo and Juliet*. *Much Ado About Nothing* and *As You Like It* date from the same period as the political drama *Henry V*. Professor Farnham may well declare that the evolution from *Julius Caesar* to *Hamlet* illustrates an intensification of interior suffering, but in so doing he is overlooking the fact that between the two Shakespeare wrote *The Merry Wives of Windsor*. Professor Charlton can demonstrate that *Macbeth* marks the beginning of a moral conscience lacking in the characters of *King Lear*. Yet we are not at all sure which of the two was written first. Robert Speaight finds a degeneration of values in *Macbeth* that are still present in *Hamlet*. Who would believe that a farce such as *Twelfth Night* was written during the period of this metamorphosis? And what logic is there to the fairy plays that marked the end of his career? Is it possible that Prospero's 'drowning his book' symbolizes Shakespeare's retirement from the theatre? And is it reasonable to believe that the poet, at the height of his fame, decided to crown his sublime masterpieces with the sublime platitudes of *Henry VIII?*

We are thus forced to reject the traditional image of a comic writer turning to politics, of a political dramatist then turning to philosophy and finally, by a supreme avatar, attaining the serenity of a sage. It is quite true that a comic vein predominated during the poet's early years, an interest in history marked his maturity, and that he was especially preoccupied with tragedy in his later period. And yet the order of the plays' composition is such as to preclude any logical classification into neat categories. In spite of Philip Sydney's sarcasms, the idea of categories was alien to the Elizabethan age. Should *The Merchant of Venice* be classed as comedy, or *Measure for Measure* as drama? No division here interrupts the thread of existence. The most hilarious interlude links the crime to the punishment. As in *Hamlet*, laments are seasoned with puns. There is no tragedy without a smile, and vice versa, no pleasure without sorrow. In *As You Like It*, Jaques' melancholy and the suffering of the old Duke in exile act as foils for the gaiety of the other couples; in *The Comedy of Errors* the threat of death weighs heavily on Aegeon; and death itself suddenly interrupts the jests of *Love's Labour's Lost*. But if the differences among all these plays are not so great as we tend to believe, it is because there is a basic unity underlying every circumstance, every expression:

Why is my verse so barren of new pride,
So far from variation or quick change?
Why with the time do I not glance aside
To new-found methods and to compounds strange?[1]

Thus the most varied theatre becomes, paradoxically, the site of supreme identity. Which is another way of saying that, beneath their trappings, comedy, history, and tragedy all reveal a single secret, a single purpose.

---

[1] *Sonnet* LXXVI.

– *What is the end of study? let me know.*
– *Why, that to know which else we should not know.*
– *Things hid and barr'd, you mean, from common sense?*

Love's Labour's Lost

The Alchemistic Theatre

In England, as everywhere else, the Renaissance was accompanied by a flowering of occultism. This is but another paradox of this disconcerting age: if man had never been more concerned about his material interests, he also had never examined more intensely the supernatural. Between the collapse of medieval faith and the first modern philosophies, man's mind, threatened by its own chaos, was forced to have recourse to a transcendental wisdom. Every age marked by great change has seen similar agonies of spirit and taken similar refuge in various forms of religion, and this phenomenon would not interest us particularly were it not for the fact that it is always marked by a renewal of the dramatic conscience. Throughout history occultism and the theater have always been closely allied. After all, born of a common principle, they both work toward the same end: to restore to man, by a mystical purification, the feeling of his divinity.

It is this unknown realm of Elizabethan knowledge that today needs to be explored. Certain critics – Alfred Dodd, E. M. Tillyard, Theodore Spencer, Arnold Stein, D. S. Savage, Paul Arnold – have already laid the groundwork. 'To renounce the things of this world, to struggle towards light, to search for heaven and the celestial breath, these are the aspirations of Sydney and his whole

87

age,' says Arnold. Without mentioning such well-known alchemistic works as those of Samuel Norton, Thomas Harriot, or
Edward Kelly, most Elizabethan writings reflect this quest for
the absolute, this reawakening of a tradition which, through
secret societies, goes back to the ancient mysteries. Thus Lyly's
Endimion applies the theories of Johann Tritheim and Cornelius
Agrippa; Sydney's *Astrophel and Stella* describe a veritable mystic
itinerary; in a 'letter to his love', the Earl of Northumberland
extols, in the manner of Alhazan's *Optic*, 'the knowledge which
alone prepares us for eternal joys and leads
us to the heart of hidden secrets'; Spenser's
Faerie Queene and Marlowe's *Faustus*
are steeped in neoplatonic reminiscences;
Nashe's *Pierce Penilesse* makes use of
Picturius' demonology; Thomas Heywood
makes up a *Hierarchy of the Blessed Angels*
based on the various stages of the cabala;
Chapman's *Hymns* to Cynthia and to Night
are inspired by gnostic philosophy, etc.[1]
Finally, we need hardly stress the role
that was played in this culture by the
ideas of Marsile Ficin, Nicholas de Cuse,
Pico della Mirandola, and by the greatest
alchemist of them all, Paracelsus.

It is worth noting that the rulers
themselves were the first to take an interest
in the occult and the strange. We know
that Elizabeth, an ardent devotee of
spiritualism, supported the astrologer John
Dee, whose angelic visitations were used to
determine the most propitious occasions
for various undertakings, throughout her
long career. She herself was prone to
fits of mysticism, and they tended to become
increasingly neurotic as she grew older.
During her final illness she consulted the
astral situation on January 24, 1603, and
was advised to keep away from Whitehall
and go to live at Richmond. At Whitehall,

---

[1] Paul Arnold: 'Elizabethan Occultism,' *Cahiers
du Sud*, 1951, no. 308.

Faust: a picture of sorcery.

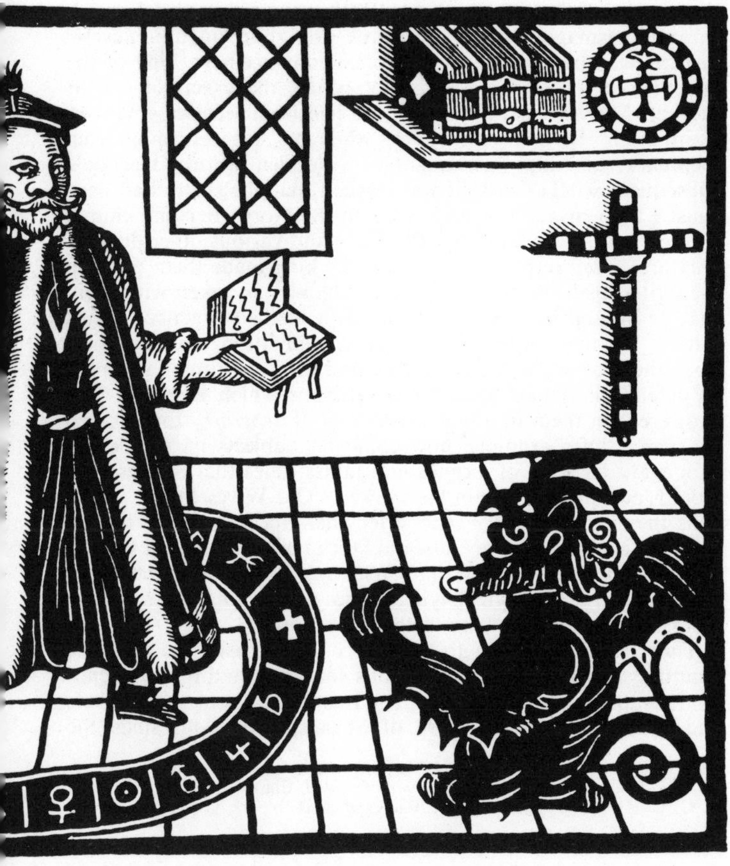

moreover, a series of baleful visions had warned her of her approaching end: her own body, 'exceedingly lean and fearful', had appeared to her in the bright flames of fire. At Richmond the visions recurred, and her ladies-in-waiting were witness to her hallucinations. On her deathbed she took part in a session of necromancy and exorcism, and one night a lady-in-waiting, having just left the queen asleep in her room, met her four rooms away. Returning in haste to the queen's bedchamber, she found Elizabeth still fast asleep. On another occasion a playing card, the Queen of Hearts, was found with a nail driven through the forehead, fastened to the bottom of the queen's chair.[1] With the succession of James I, this phantasmagoric atmosphere grew even more intense. Several disturbing experiences had long since convinced the king of the effectiveness of satanism. Shortly before the execution of his mother, Mary Stuart, a bloody head had been seen winging over Edinburgh. Several years later, while he was returning from Denmark, his ship was caught in a sudden storm. During a subsequent witches' trial it was learned that the storm had been caused by a mystic rite performed in the North Berwick church by a certain Agnes Simpson, Dr. Fian, and various other diabolic creatures. Before passing sentence, the king made them perform their rites again in his presence, and he was so taken with them that he himself became an ardent adept of their practices. Thus during his reign astrology, alchemy, divination, and cabalism flourished to such a degree that we find the king himself stooping to defend charlatans against the sarcasms which Reginald Scot showered on them in *The Discoverie of Witchcraft*. Encouraged by such a lofty example, how could his subjects have failed to propagate all sorts of legends and fables, tales that Shakespeare would later incorporate in his work? '"Old Wives Fables", Ady calls them, writing forty years after Shakespeare's death, told as they sit "chatting of many false old Stories of Witches, and Fairies, and Robin Good-Fellow, and Walking Spirits, and the Dead walking again; all of which lying fancies people are more naturally inclined to listen after than to the Scriptures". '[2]

Thus from the throne to the tavern, from castles to cottages, countless superstitions provided this society with ample evidence of the supernatural. Few works tell us more about these beliefs and practices than do those of Shakespeare. And since the

---

[1] J.-H. Rosny, Jr.: *Elizabeth, Queen of England*, Flammarion, 1929, p. 126.
[2] G. L. Kittredge: *The Complete Works of Shakespeare*, Ginn, p. 229.

mystical world makes little distinction between human and animal, we begin with an enumeration of a fabulous bestiary:

Jesus in Hell: a picture of exorcism.

> *I cannot choose: sometimes he angers me*
> *With telling me of the moldwarp and the ant,*
> *Of the dreamer Merlin and his prophecies,*
> *And of a dragon, and a finless fish,*
> *A clip-wing'd griffin, and a moulton raven,*
> *A couching lion, and a rambling cat,*
> *And such a deal of skimble-skamble stuff*
> *As puts me from my faith.* [1]

Animals that are either maleficent or good, imaginary or real, heraldic or vile, charming or monstrous, straightway form an integral part of this dramatic repertory. Tigers, wolves, vultures,

---

[1] *Henry IV, Part 1*, III, 1, 147–155.

and serpents in *King Lear;* dogs, asses, camels, and horses in *Troilus and Cressida;* birds in *A Midsummer Night's Dream* and *The Tempest,* all derive from a symbolism of grace or repulsion which constantly accompanies and reinforces the plot. Botany also furnishes its share of emblematic images, such as the flowers that Ophelia distributes to the witnesses of her madness: rosemary, fennel, violets, columbine, rue, marigolds, pansies, and daisies; or those that Perdita distributes to the guests at the sheep-shearing feast: carnations, stock, lavender, mints, savory, marjoram, lilies, jonquils, primroses.... It would seem that in this world every person and thing partakes of the same secret order of efficacy, from the plants whose juices Brother Lawrence praises in *Romeo and Juliet* to the ingredients from which the witches extract their philtres in *Macbeth.* The majority of Shakespearean metaphors thus derive from some fantastic flora or fauna whose qualities are defined by their resemblance to our moods. Fear has its snakes, anger its wild animals, love its fruits, madness its tares:

> *Alack ! 'tis he: why, he was met even now*
> *As mad as the vex'd sea; singing aloud;*
> *Crown'd with rank fumiter and furrow weeds,*
> *With burdocks, hemlock, nettles, cuckoo-flowers,*
> *Darnel, and all the idle weeds that grow*
> *In our sustaining corn.*[1]

Owls, vipers, unicorns, or mandrake thus exist only to represent our terrors, our desires, and, from sign to sign, to determine our destiny. Seen in this light, the whole world constantly reflects the disorder of our instincts.

Thus superstition lends much more than an atmosphere or philosophy to Shakespeare's plays. An unbroken chain of relationships links the universe to man, man to the universe. Everything is a symbol, and each symbol has power over its object. The very presence of a corpse on board a ship suffices to unleash a storm, as the passage of a murderer is enough to make his victim's body bleed. What is more, if all levels of reality merge and are interdependent, nothing can be fortuitous, and every eclipse, every apparition, every conjunction of clouds and colors is immediately taken as a sign or an oracle:

---

[1] *King Lear*, IV, 4, 1–6.

> *'Tis thought the king is dead: we will not stay.*
> *The bay trees in our country are all wither'd*
> *And meteors fright the fixed stars of heaven,*
> *And pale-fac'd moon looks bloody on the earth*
> *And lean-look'd prophets whisper fearful change . . .*
> *These signs forerun the death or fall of kings.*[1]

This is why, in *Julius Caesar*, *King John*, and *Richard III*, crimes go hand in hand with plagues and calamities. This is why, in *Cymbeline* and *The Tempest*, clemency tends to pacify the elements. This is why, in *Henry VI* or in *Hamlet*, man discovers he has the power of communicating with demons and ghosts. Here the world and the soul interpenetrate. With *Macbeth* and *King Lear*, analogy turns to identity: the storm speaks through the ravings of the old king, as war through the prophecies of the witches, and the forest marches against the usurper. The hero's fate is thus integrated in an immense metamorphosis of creation: transcending any actor, encompassing his cosmic liberty, the word translates human tragedy in the language of winds, fire, stars, and seas.

All these beliefs were to find their ultimate expression in the Rosicrucian philosophy, which was introduced into England at the time of Shakespeare's greatest plays. Certain concordances discovered by Paul Arnold between Spenser's *Faerie Queene* and the work of one of the founders of the Rosicrucian sect, *The Chemical Nuptials*, by Johan Valentin Andreae, lead us to believe that the themes of this mystical theology were already known to early Elizabethans. 'The identity of the two symbols – Spenser's and Andreae's – is absolute, and we cannot for a moment doubt that the two texts, neither of which could feasibly have influenced the other, are two versions of the same occult tradition.'[2] Be that as it may, the honor of having revealed the Rosicrucian mysteries to the English belongs to the fabulous Robert Fludd. The doctrine he was to expound, particularly in his *Summum Bonum*, is based on that of Paracelsus and also can be found in the writings of Michael Maier, Jacob Boehme, and the early theoreticians of Freemasonry. Which means that it stems from the most authentic of hermetic traditions. All this would scarcely be worth mentioning were it not for the fact that, by a strange quirk of fate, it also constitutes Shakespeare's philosophy.

---

[1]   *Richard II*, II, 4, 7–15.
[2]   Paul Arnold, *op. cit.*

In the beginning, says Fludd, there reigned that unity which the cabala calls the 'Ain Soph': the nothingness, the unknowable, the absolute. All creation derived from it, by a series of divisions, the first of which engendered Being. God, having materialized from the void, reveals Himself to Himself and, enigmatically, separates the two principles that religions describe: the *voluntas*, an active, luminous, masculine principle, and the *noluntas*, a passive, shadowy, feminine principle. From the copulation of these opposites, whose distinction preceded time, is born primeval matter, chaos, and by progressive differentiations, the three substances: – sulphur, mercury, and salt – the four elements, and, finally, the beings and things which form the reign of the multiple. At the conclusion of this triple emanation, nature, animals, and men make up the lowest level of a reality whose summit is lost in the eternal. Whence the necessity for a saving metamorphosis: death, which, dissolving matter, frees the divine fire which dwells therein. Like Jesus, our flesh will die to give birth to the spirit. Creation, fall, resurrection are thus the three acts of a universal drama everywhere repeated, from the cycle of the seasons to the succession of kings. This is why man seems endowed with an essentially historic mission: to assume here below this movement from a fallen state to redemption. The theatrical catharsis seeks to attain the very goal of occultism: for by symbolically inflicting death upon us, tragedy, like the initiation, resurrects us, summarizes in us the story of the cosmos which, born of God, must return to God when time will have run its course.

Ironically, it is *The Comedy of Errors* which propounds for us this concept of the genesis and the end. There is no play in all Shakespeare with a better title, since the error would be precisely to think of it as a comedy. From the very start the ideal cosmological problem is presented: the formation of the multiple which will be resolved by the final revelation. Two cities, Ephesus and Syracuse, are at war, thus symbolizing the first rupture of unity. And, as though he were relating the creation of the world, the poet informs us, through the voice of Aegeon, of the successive avatars of this principle. Once the merchant Aegeon and his wife Aemilia lived happily at Syracuse:

> So they lov'd, as love in twain
> Had the essence but in one;
> Two distincts, divisions none.[1]

---

[1] *The Phoenix and the Turtle*, 25–27.

Their fortunes prospered, and all would have been well except for the intervention of an unlucky star. Forced by the death of one of his factors to leave home and take charge of the '*goods at random left*', Aegeon tears himself away from the '*kind embracements of his spouse*', and goes to Epidamnum. Six months later Aemilia rejoins him and gives birth to twins on the very same day that a '*meaner woman*' is delivered of male twins in the selfsame inn. Filled with pity, Aegeon buys these boys, whose surname is Dromio, intending that they should later become attendants to his own two sons, Antipholus of Ephesus and Antipholus of Syracuse. On their way home their ship is wrecked and split in two by a storm. Aegeon, one of his sons, and one of the Dromio boys are rescued by another ship and later return to Syracuse; Aemilia, her other son, and the other Dromio boy are picked up by a different vessel and brought to Ephesus. Eighteen years later Antipholus and Dromio of Syracuse decide to set out in search of their brothers. Five years pass; tired of waiting, Aegeon sets out after them. Fate brings these wanderers to Ephesus, where Aegeon, as a native of Syracuse, is arrested and condemned to death. However, moved by Aegeon's tale of woe, the authorities grant him a day's reprieve to find his sons and '*seek his life by beneficial help*'. If he fails, the executioner will carry out the sentence. And, of course, after numerous misunderstandings, Antipholus recognizes Antipholus; Dromio, Dromio; Aegeon, Aemilia. And the family, at last united, will be restored to its former harmony.

This story, secretly mathematical, relates a series of disasters, each of which seems marked by the rupture of a couple. The action progresses here as the universe in Hesiod's *Theogony*. The initial separation of husband and wife corresponds, in the cabala, to the separation of the *voluntas* and *noluntas*, these two powers which, throughout time, will try to come together again, to reform their original unity. But then the double gives birth to the quadruple: the two Antipholus and the two Dromios, about whom it can be said that '*an apple cleft in two is not more twin than these two creatures*'.[1] Then a third division occurs and disrupts the coherence of the whole, scattering father, mother, brothers, and attendants in a symbolic shipwreck. It is here that the unity reaches its point of maximum division and gives way to the multiple, that is, to error and illusion:

---

[1] *Twelfth Night*, V, 1, 233–234.

> *And here we wander in illusions:*
> *Some blessed power deliver us from hence!...*
> *O, for my beads! I cross me for a sinner.*
> *This is the fairy land: O! spite of spites.*
> *We talk with goblins, owls, and elvish sprites.*[1]

But man must deliver himself from this confusion or perish, and the death sentence hanging over Aegeon clearly shows us that this danger is very real. Thus we find all these characters feverishly searching for one another and deeply longing for their lost unity:

> *I to the world am like a drop of water*
> *That in the ocean seeks another drop;*
> *Who, falling there to find his fellow forth,*
> *Unseen, inquisitive, confounds himself.*

This nostalgia for 'union', as well as for 'knowledge', is again expressed in Antipholus of Syracuse's first words to Luciana:

> *Sweet mistress, – what your name is else, I know not,*
> *Nor by what wonder you do hit of mine, –*
> *Less in your knowledge and your grace you show not*
> *Than our earth's wonder; more than earth divine.*
> *Teach me, dear creature, how to think and speak:*
> *Lay open to my earthy-gross conceit,*
> *Smother'd in errors, feeble, shallow, weak,*
> *The folded meaning of your words' deceit.*
> *Against my soul's pure truth why labour you*
> *To make it wander in an unknown field?*
> *Are you a god? would you create me new?*

It is evident that finding one's likeness means not only re-discovering one's identity, but participating in an actual transmutation of existence. Once the errors are dispelled, by a sort of mechanism similar to that which assures the victory of summer over winter, all these people recognize each other and unity is reestablished. At the end the family is reunited in the same order that circumstance had divided it, and since this reunion implies a 'new birth', Aemilia concludes:

---

[1] *The Comedy of Errors*, IV, 3, 42–43; II, 2, 190–192; I, 2, 35–40; III, 2, 29–39; V, 1, 403–405.

Thirty-three years have I but gone in travail
Of you, my sons; and till this present hour
My heavy burdens ne'er delivered.

This work, one of Shakespeare's earliest, contains the basic pattern of his entire theatre. The divorce of the masculine and feminine recurs in fact both in *Pericles* and *As You Like It*, and results in a series of misunderstandings analogous to those that beset the Ephesians and Syracusians. As for *A Midsummer Night's Dream*, 'this is a new comedy of errors,' says Paul Reyher, 'but much richer than the first, in that it includes the elements and the spirit world, and very different too, for here the extraordinary, the philtres and charms, fairies and sprites are not illusive, but pervade the entire play.'[1] And here too the conflict of major principles, incarnated by Oberon and Titania, plunges the mortals into darkness and aberrations which only the reconciliation of the gods and heroes dispels. We find the same situation in *Cymbeline*, where the unity sealed by the secret marriage of Imogen and Posthumus, and broken by the treachery of the Queen and Iachimo, is restored in the end and embellished by the twins, Guiderius and Arviragus. Similarly, in *The Winter's Tale*, two kings '*trained together in their childhood*' become enemies and are reconciled only with the marriage of their children, Florizel and Perdita, symbolized by the resurrection of Hermione. Thus in the fairy-plays, as well as in the comedies, a group of people united by the ties of love suddenly find themselves separated and try gropingly, through discords and sorrows, to recreate this unity, the cosmic and metaphysical meaning of which cannot be doubted. As a final example, witness the end of *The Tempest*:

In one voyage
Did Claribel her husband find at Tuinis,
And Ferdinand, her brother, found a wife
Where he himself was lost; Prospero his dukedom
In a poor isle; and all of us ourselves,
When no man was his own.[2]

Seen in this light, a comedy as seemingly banal as *The Two Gentlemen of Verona* reveals, as it unfolds, a real initiative method. Two friends take leave of each other in the first scene of Act I.

[1]   Paul Reyher: *An Essay on the Ideas in the Work of Shakespeare*, Didier, 1947, p. 164.
[2]   *The Tempest*, V, 1, 208–213.

Proteus, in love with Julia, remains in Verona to court her, while Valentine, the *adventurous* soul, leaves for Milan '*to see the wonders of the world*', assuring his friend that '*home-keeping youth have ever homely wits*'. Thus in the beginning of the alchemistic legends, and especially in Andreae's *The Chemical Nuptials*, the adept sets out without a clear idea of his goal. At least the purity of his ambitions will serve him as a viaticum and, with a bit of good luck, a miraculous instinct will keep him out of trouble. Such will be the fate of Valentine, and the love he jokes about is the one Proteus will suddenly refute shortly thereafter: that profane love which, acting as an obstacle rather than a fulfillment, keeps Proteus from the pursuit of knowledge:

> *Thou, Julia, thou hast metamorphos'd me;*
> *Made me neglect my studies, lose my time,*
> *War with good counsel, set the world at nought;*
> *Made wit with musing weak, heart sick with thought.*

With this confession a whole world separates our two gentlemen: Valentine demands a full, authentic life; Proteus is the lover who regrets having loved, a mediocre person whom passion impoverishes rather then ennobles. His mistress, Julia, also seems strangely given to coquetry. Incapable of real surrender, she tears up her suitor's letters and then, a moment later, gathers up the pieces; and in the presence of her waiting maid, Lucetta, she willingly disparages the attachment that secretly obsesses her. But it so happens that the lovers are to be separated and the friends reunited, for Proteus' father, tired of seeing his son languish at Verona, sends him to be educated at the Court of Milan which, by its refinement and the quality of its hosts, recalls the castle of Belmont in *The Merchant of Venice* and that of the *Chemical Nuptials of Christian Rosenkreutz*. Upon his arrival at this seat of higher learning Proteus finds Valentine already transformed, enamored of Sylvia, and tormented not to know that she requites his love. Their meeting takes place in the presence of this exceptional woman and Proteus, straightway forgetting his Julia, falls madly in love with her. And it is here that the opposition between the two characters is finally revealed, for while Valentine, a generous person, extols his compatriot's virtues, Proteus wastes no time betraying his friend by informing the Duke of his plans '*to steal Sylvia away*'. Thus while one follows the path of love, the other chooses hypocrisy and perjury. Both by slandering Valentine and declaring his love to Sylvia, Proteus shows himself to be equally base, and this is why his hopes are doomed to fail miserably. For who is Sylvia?

VALENTINE. *Is she not a heavenly saint?*
PROTEUS. *No, but she is an earthly paragon.*
VALENTINE. *Call her divine.*

or, '*if not divine, yet let her be a principality sovereign to all the creatures on the earth.*' A mystic would use much the same terms, and Proteus himself will soon adopt the tone:

> *Who is Sylvia? what is she,*
> *That all our swains commend her?*
> *Holy, fair, and wise is she;*
> *The heaven such grace did lend her,*
> *That she might admired be.* etc.

This song certainly reveals the influence of courtly love, which was also the inspiration for the idylls of *Love's Labour's Lost*, but the works of Denis de Rougemont have shown us to what extent this love transcended the person of the beloved and aimed at celestial perfection, ultimate knowledge. There can be no doubt but that saintliness, charity, and wisdom here make of Sylvia, as of Andreae's Virgin, the person through whom one is initiated into the 'philosophical wonders' that Valentine is burning to discover. The last stanza is quite specific:

> *Then to Sylvia let us sing,*
> *That Sylvia is excelling;*
> *She excels each mortal thing*
> *Upon the dull earth dwelling;*
> *To her let us garlands bring.*

Nevertheless, Proteus' treachery succeeds and Valentine, banished by the angry Duke, laments his fate like a good Christian deprived of grace:

> *What light is light if Sylvia be not seen?*
> *What joy is joy if Sylvia be not by?...*
> *She is my essence; and I leave to be,*
> *If I be not by her fair influence*
> *Foster'd, illumin'd, cherish'd, kept alive.*

Separated from his beloved, the adept now begins his period of trial. Like Rosenkreutz surprising Venus asleep, he has been allowed to contemplate perfection, and now he must win it.

99

Banned, we find him wandering in a forest, where he is captured by some operetta-like bandits, who straightway make him their chief. But as adversity ennobles Valentine, his foil Proteus wallows in vileness, to the point of serving as go-between for the scurvy Thurio. Against these intrigues, Sylvia's sarcasms recall the imprecations with which the Virgin of the *Nuptials* showers those audacious souls who aspire to the Great Work without first having achieved the necessary moral qualities:

> *For me, by this pale queen of night I swear,*
> *I am so far from granting thy request*
> *That I despise thee for thy wrongful suit.*

Then the infamous Proteus, since Sylvia will give him nothing better, begs her for her '*picture for my love, the picture that is hanging in your chamber.*' In itself this request further clarifies the plot: if Valentine, in spite of his trials and tribulations, moves toward the attainment of his goal, Proteus on the other hand represents the man who has taken the wrong road and is henceforth content with shoddy substitutes. Does he not admit it?

> *I am but a shadow*
> *And to your shadow will I make true love.*

The final act: under the auspicious sign of the sun that '*begins to gild the western sky*', the two lovers will be reunited, the mystic union consummated. While the Duke, Thurio, Proteus, and Julia hunt for one other and lose their way in the forest – symbolizing those who, lacking knowledge, pursue it like the blind in the dark of night – Valentine and Sylvia go straight to each other, as if attracted by a magic force. And the last scene, the regeneration, witnesses their exchange of pardons and oaths, as the reconciled couples make preparations for the wedding:

> *That done, our day of marriage shall be yours;*
> *One feast, one house, one mutual happiness.*[1]

Thus Shakespearean erotica derives both from the secret philosophy of the troubadours and the allegorical moral of the alchemists. From *Romeo and Juliet* to *Pericles*, from *As You Like It* to *The Winter's Tale*, the woman is exalted as the symbol of a

---

[1] *The Two Gentlemen of Verona*, I, 1, 66–69; II, 4, 146–154; IV, 2, 40–54; III, 1, 173–184; IV, 2, 103–105; IV, 2, 127–128; V, 4, 172–173.

status that man must win by constancy, chastity, and renunciation. At least this is true in the cases of Beatrice, Rosalind, Helen, Juliet, and especially Hermione, Paulina, and Perdita who, to counteract the jealousy, obstinacy, and cruelty of Leontes, employ the triple arms of fidelity, goodness, and grace. Seen from this point of view, the conquest of a woman seems to be nothing more than the inferior, exoteric aspect of the attainment of a divine condition. It presupposes an asceticism comparable to the quest for the Holy Grail, rites of initiation, and various degrees of the Work, the last of which, the marriage of mercury and sulphur, is in fact entitled: the marriage of the King and Queen. But nowhere is the mystic meaning of this union better illustrated than in the denouement of *Love's Labour's Lost*, where, to achieve final grace, the postulant must submit to a period of retreat and meditation:

> *But go with speed*
> *To some forlorn and naked hermitage,*
> *Remote from all the pleasures of the world;*
> *There stay, until the twelve celestial signs*
> *Have brought about their annual reckoning.*
> *If this austere insociable life*
> *Change not your offer made in heat of blood;*
> *If frosts and fasts, hard lodging and thin weeds,*
> *Nip not the gaudy blossoms of your love,*
> *But that it bear this trial and last love;*
> *Then, at the expiration of the year*
> *Come challenge me, challenge me by these deserts,*
> *And, by this virgin palm now kissing thine,*
> *I will be thine.*[1]

In *The Merchant of Venice* this same process of redeeming initiation is again exemplified. The two plots – Antonio's debt and noble Portia's love – slowly fuse into a single theme: the act of charity which, when it finally occurs, will save those who are worthy of it. Corresponding to these two episodes are two different settings where the action unfolds: Venice, the city of lucre and sensual appetites, and Belmont, the real castle of the Grail, where Portia, having rid herself of two suitors, must give in to the third, Bassanio. The story begins in the commercial sectors of the city and ends in the gardens of the manor, thus symbolizing the

---

[1]   *Love's Labour's Lost*, V, 2, 802–815.

evolution from commerce to nobility, debauchery to purity, from the vulgar to the spiritual life.

This transmutation appears most clearly in the famous casket scenes. It goes without saying that Portia, like Hermione or Sylvia, symbolizes the ultimate love, the ultimate wisdom that man can hope for in this life:

> *Why, that's the lady: all the world desires her;*
> *From the four corners of the earth they come,*
> *To kiss this shrine, this mortal-breathing saint:*
> *The Hyrcanian deserts and the vasty wilds*
> *Of wide Arabia are as thoroughfares now*
> *For princes to come view fair Portia.*[1]

But Portia, if she is to be courted, intends to bestow her hand only on him who successfully passes a test similar to that the young Pericles will have to pass:

> *Before thee stands this fair Hesperides,*
> *With golden fruit, but dangerous to be touch'd;*
> *For death-like dragons here affright thee hard:*
> *Her face, like heaven, enticeth thee to view*
> *Her countless glory, which desert must gain;*
> *And which, without desert, because thine eye*
> *Presumes to reach, all thy whole heap must die.*[2]

The three suitors must choose from among three caskets of gold, silver, and lead, one of which contains the 'celestial image' of their idol. The alchemists' tales frequently portrayed the adept at a crossroads, from which only one road leads to salvation, and here Shakespeare seems to vulgarize the parable by substituting the traditional metals of the alchemists. What does the gold casket say? '*Who chooseth me shall gain what many men desire.*' That is, death, for to choose gold is to prefer material wealth to the riches of the soul and, consequently, to be dead to the only joys that matter. As a punishment for his error the Prince of Morocco finds only '*a carrion Death*' inside, a skeleton; from Portia he receives '*a gentle riddance*'. The silver casket bears the inscription: '*Who chooseth me shall get as much as he deserves.*' But what does one whose life is not completely dedicated to the pursuit of knowledge deserve? Nothing but base humiliation, and this is

---

[1]   *The Merchant of Venice*, II, 7, 38–43.
[2]   *Pericles, Prince of Tyre*, I, 1, 27–33.

The most excellent

Historie of the *Merchant* of *Venice*.

VVith the extreame crueltie of *Shylocke* the Iewe
towards the sayd Merchant, in cutting a iust pound
of his flesh: and the obtayning of *Portia*
by the choyse of three
chests.

As it hath beene diuers times acted by the Lord
Chamberlaine his Seruants.

Written by William Shakespeare.

AT LONDON,
Printed by *I. R.* for Thomas Heyes,
and are to be sold in Paules Church-yard, at the
signe of the Greene Dragon.
1600.

Changling   Simpleton

Sr I. Falstafe   Clause

Hostes

precisely what the Prince of Arragon gets when he opens the silver casket: '*the portrait of a blinking idiot*' presenting him a scroll of enigmatic adages dealing with the treatment of metals. Finally, the lead casket, on which is written: '*Who chooseth me must give and hazard all he hath.*' This is the third way, the narrow gate, the *via regia* of sacrifice. In choosing it Bassanio wins Portia: he changes the base lead of appearances into the gold of revelation. And his victory straightway propels him beyond the limits of human nature into a paradise '*where every something, being blent together, turns to a wild of nothing, save of joy, express'd and not express'd.*'

The esoteric moral of *The Merchant of Venice* therefore confirms that of *The Two Gentlemen of Verona.* Like Valentine, Bassanio only achieves mastery through adversity and total submission. But these chosen few are more than ever confronted by the opposition of the world of the blind. The differences separating Proteus and Valentine are not so great as those that separate Shylock and Portia. Like Faust, Antonio has signed Shylock's loan by agreeing to repay it with a pound of his own flesh. When the debt falls due, Shylock drags Antonio to a court of justice presided over by Portia disguised as a judge, as the Duke of Vienna presides in *Measure for Measure.* It soon becomes evident that the deceit was indeed premeditated. Two worlds here meet head on, like heaven and hell, with Antonio between them symbolizing mankind, the stake. If Portia incarnates the virtues of generosity, grandeur, and beauty, Shylock on the other hand symbolizes the corresponding vices. With the law on his side, he shows himself to be the implacable calculator, the cynic who demands his due, whose sense of justice scorns all mercy:

> *The quality of mercy is not strain'd,*
> *It droppeth as the gentle rain from heaven*
> *Upon the place beneath: it is twice bless'd;*
> *It blesseth him that gives and him that takes:*
> *'Tis mightiest in the mightiest;...*
> *And earthly power doth then show likest God's*
> *When mercy seasons justice. Therefore, Jew,*
> *Though justice be thy plea, consider this,*
> *That in the course of justice none of us*
> *Should see salvation...* [1]

---

[1] *The Merchant of Venice*, IV, 1, 184–200.

In order to give the play its full meaning, the demands of law must give way to the duty of love. The most subtle dialectic will not only deprive Shylock of his pound of flesh, but also, by turning his accusations against him, will bring about his ruin. In the process the defendant, Antonio, becomes the champion of the worthy cause. Portia, whose role as an initiator is firmly established, secures his pardon and thus frees him, as she freed Bassanio, from his final bondage. But had not Antonio, by his initial sacrifice, started off on the right road? Prison and the trial were sufficient proof of his constancy. As a final proof – one which, as a matter of fact, occurs in the masonic rites of initiation – Antonio, like Hamlet, had felt the 'bare bodkin' pressed against his breast. Victorious, he in turn can enter the ideal temple at Belmont and, under the aegis of Portia, found a sort of lodge together with Bassanio, Lorenzo, Gratiano, Jessica, and Nerissa, a superior society governed only by the laws of poetry and music.

Music. It is everywhere in Shakespeare. It wanders like some lordly master between the stars and men. Its medium is night and wonder its instrument. From its depths prophetic dreams are born, destiny emerges, the dead reappear:

> *But, what music?*
> *My lord, I hear none.*
> *None! The music of the spheres!... Most heavenly music:*
> *It nips me unto list'ning, and thick slumber*
> *Hangs upon mine eyes.*[1]

and then the moon brightens the horizon of a darkened sky to preside, as in times past, over the orphic mysteries:

> *Now, fair Hippolyta, our nuptial hour*
> *Draws on apace: four happy days bring in*
> *Another moon; but O! methinks how slow*
> *This old moon wanes.*

This moon, under whose sign the final scene of *The Merchant of Venice* unfolds, reveals the cosmic mechanism of initiation in *A Midsummer Night's Dream*. It reappears at various intervals to illuminate, as the tale progresses, the path of those in search of the absolute. Described as 'waning' in the opening scene, it will complete a full cycle, from death to resurrection, toward that new moon which will sanctify the marriage of the King and Queen:

---

[1]   *Pericles*, V, 1, 228–236.

> *Four days will quickly steep themselves in night;*
> *For nights will quickly dream away the time;*
> *And then the moon, like to a silver bow*
> *New bent in heaven, shall behold the night*
> *Of our solemnities.*

On this same night the rebel Hermia will be executed if she refuses to marry Demetrius:

> *Take time to pause; and, by the next new moon, –*
> *The sealing-day betwixt my love and me*
> *For everlasting bond of fellowship, –*
> *Upon that day either prepare to die*
> *For disobedience to your father's will,*
> *Or else to wed Demetrius.*

We can easily see what a close bond exists between love, dream, and death, three states that mortals must experience before being initiated to the light of salvation. Until that deliverance a time of anxiety will reign, which Oberon and Titania feel responsible for:

> *Therefore the moon, the governess of floods,*
> *Pale in her anger, washes all the air,*
> *That rheumatic diseases do abound.*

Similarly, Theseus' kingdom is plagued by floods, sterility, downpours, and epidemics, and we realize that here, as around the castle of Amfortas, the earth is suffering from some sort of curse. Before the marriage rites regenerate it, the earth will continue to be governed by the influence of an ill-starred moon, the 'cold, unfertile moon' venerated by Artemis' nuns. Beneath its unkind rays Helen, Demetrius, Lysander, and Hermia vainly pursue each other. To counteract its baneful influence, Oberon vainly dispatches Puck armed with a magic potion, but either by mistake or mischievousness, the imp only aggravates the situation still further. Bewailing their fate, the lovers wander in the dark wood, Titania falls in love with the ass Bottom, the fairies quake before the shadow creatures – spotted snakes with double tongues, thorny hedgehogs, newts and blindworms, spiders and slugs – and Helen in utter desperation cries '*O! wilt thou darkling leave me? do not so*', while Hermia awakens from a dream swearing that a serpent had eaten her heart away.

As an antidote to this 'baleful planet', which perpetuates the battle between the sexes, Venus is then invoked, sitting enthroned in her clear and radiant light '*high up in her shining sphere.*' And in the thick of the drama Oberon, casting a spell on Demetrius, offers the prayer:

> *When his love he doth espy,*
> *Let her shine as gloriously*
> *As the Venus of the sky*

And magically, at the moment when the god is untangling the misunderstandings and preparing a happy ending, the star of love appears in the sky and begins to dispel the evil influence of the moon. It is high time. The quarrels have degenerated to the point of absurdity. Lysander draws his sword against Demetrius, chases Helen, insults Hermia, and utter confusion reigns as all the characters mutually accuse and curse one another. '*Lord, what fools these mortals be!*' But the good spirit is watching over them: as Ariel disperses the victims of the shipwreck through the charm of music, so Puck isolates and separates the lovers, drawing them into the gentle lap of sleep:

OBERON.　*When they next wake, all this derision*
　　　　　Shall seem a dream and fruitless vision;
　　　　　And back to Athens shall the lovers wend,
　　　　　With league whose date till death shall never end...
　　　　　and all things shall be in peace.
PUCK.　*My fairy lord, this must be done with haste,*
　　　　　For night's swift dragons cut the clouds full fast,
　　　　　And yonder shines Aurora's harbinger;
　　　　　At whose approach, ghosts, wandering here and there,
　　　　　Troop home to churchyards: damned spirits all,
　　　　　That in cross-ways and floods have burial,
　　　　　Already to their wormy beds have gone.

The ill-starred reign of the moon is drawing to a close. Morning will soon exorcise the spell by the alchemy of the sun which, rising from the sea '*all fiery red... Turns into yellow gold his salt green stream.*' Then, speaking through the voice of Helena, the whole of nature begs for its release:

> *O weary night! O long and tedious night,*
> *Abate thy hours! shine, comforts, from the east!*

so that each can return to Theseus' palace to celebrate the redeeming marriage and bury the old moon—as an effigy is burned at Mardi Gras. For thus the summer's night must end, in joy and purity of light. This whole metamorphosis is recalled for us at random in the allegory of Pyramus and Thisby which gaily crowns the festivities:

ENTREATY

O grim-look'd night ! O night with hue so black !
O night which ever art when day is not !

APPARITION

This lanthorn doth the horned moon present;
Myself the man i' the moon do seem to be.

INCANTATION

I am weary of this moon: would he would change !
It appears by his small light of discretion,
that he is in the wane.

TRANSMUTATION

Sweet moon, I thank thee for thy sunny beams;
I thank thee moon for shining now so bright.[1]

These four plays, like many others, prove that Shakespearean comedy was actually the vehicle for philosophical problems which recur in the histories and tragedies. Even in his earliest efforts Shakespeare seems to be fully cognizant of a tradition which was to guide him in the choice and treatment of his subjects to the end of his career. Speculations about the destiny of man can lead to speculations about the destiny of dynasties; the process which regulates the phases of the moon can also apply to that which governs the phases of history. In his comedies as well as in his interpretation of the past Shakespeare means always to teach an asceticism which leads from darkness and dissension to unity and light.

Each of his historical plays begins in the midst of some corrupt situation which symbolizes both man's fallen state and the matter with which the occultists were concerned. The whole plan of action consists of evolving from this stage of perdition to one of salvation, generally associated with the triumph of justice. Such is the task of time, of that time which is always profoundly am-

---

[1] *A Midsummer Night's Dream,* I, 1, 1–4; I, 1, 7–11; I, 1, 83–88; II, 1, 103–105; III, 2, 105–107; III, 2, 370–384; III, 2, 393; III, 2, 431–432; V, 1, 171–280.

biguous. Upon occasion it is '*misshapen Time, copesmate of ugly night*' which '*murderest all there are*', and yet its glory is '*to calm contending kings, to unmask falsehood and bring truth to light.*'[1] From these conflicting functions there results, from a social point of view, the struggle between those in power and those seeking to attain it. From *King John* to *Richard III*, most of the monarchs are portrayed as either criminals or weaklings, so that the temptation to overthrow them is soon implanted in the minds of the people around them. Little by little a group of rebels is formed: ruined nobles, famous soldiers, ambitious brothers, whose fortune lends weight to their claim and nourishes their power. Disorder then takes hold of the kingdom: discord, treachery, sedition, and murder multiply till finally the opposing factions meet to determine whether misfortune or harmony will be the country's fate. So,

> *All's well that ends well: still the fine's the crown.*[2]

With the coronation of the victor, a whole people seems suddenly raised from the dead – and, in fact, the splendor of a ceremony obligingly described in detail and commented on, is sufficient evidence of the transcendental importance of the event, an occasion in which the whole of nature participates:

> *To solemnize this day the glorious sun*
> *Stays in his course and plays the alchemist,*
> *Turning with splendour of his precious eye*
> *The meagre cloddy earth to glittering gold.*[3]

But, by a similar concordance, the system which determines each particular plot also governs all of these dramas taken together as a gigantic epic. 'The entire cycle of historical plays – even including *King John*, whose very ideas make it a part of the whole – is at bottom nothing more than the history of a crime, its consequences and expiation.'[4] The crime is the overthrow and assassination of Richard II. For the Elizabethans believed that the king played a role equivalent to that of the sun in creation. Any attempt against his prerogatives sufficed to upset cosmic laws and, consequently, provoke catastrophes that certain seers were able to predict:

---

[1] *The Rape of Lucrece*, 925–929; 939–940.
[2] *All's Well that Ends Well*, IV, 4, 35.
[3] *King John*, III, 1, 77–81.
[4] Paul Reyher, *op. cit.*, p. 253.

A portrait of Ely.

> *My Lord of Hereford here, whom you call king,*
> *Is a foul traitor to proud Hereford's king;*
> *And if you crown him, let me prophesy,*
> *The blood of English shall manure the ground*
> *And future ages groan for this foul act;*
> *Peace shall go sleep with Turks and infidels,*
> *And in this seat of peace tumultuous wars*
> *Shall kin with kin and kind with kind confound;*
> *Disorder, horror, fear and mutiny'*
> *Shall here inhabit, and this land be call'd*
> *The field of Golgotha and dead men's skulls.*
> *O ! if you rear this house against this house,*
> *It will the woefullest division prove*
> *That ever fell upon this cursed earth.*
> *Prevent it, resist it, let it not be so,*
> *Lest child, child's children, cry against you 'woe !'* [1]

By usurping the throne, Bolingbroke has substituted violence for divine right. His crime brings England more disasters than all the abuses of Richard's reign would have caused. Following the fatal formula of a division – as already typified by *The Comedy of Errors* – the country splits up into two rival factions and founders in chaos under Henry VI and throughout the tyranny of Richard III. From play to play we watch the dissolution of the forms and principles of the State. Justice, authority, hierarchy, loyalty, everything is jeopardized as long as the glorious hour of redemption has not sounded. But,

> *The extreme part of time extremely forms*
> *All causes to the purpose of his speed.* [2]

And this conclusion is the restoration of the legitimate sovereignty, as a result of which the kingdom is once again blessed with peace. By reconciling the rival houses of York and Lancaster, the succession of the Tudors had logically to appear like the philosopher's stone of history, the assurance of that patiently reconquered unity:

> *England hath long been mad, and scarr'd herself;*
> *The brother blindly shed the brother's blood,*
> *The father rashly slaught'd his own son,*

---

[1] *Richard II*, IV, 1, 133–149.
[2] *Love's Labour's Lost*, V, 2, 748–749.

The son, compell'd, been butcher to the sire:
All this divided York and Lancaster,
Divided in their dire division,
O! now, let Richmond and Elizabeth,
The true succeeders of each royal house,
By God's fair ordinance conjoin together;
And let their heirs, – God, if thy will be so, –
Enrich the time to come with smooth-fac'd peace,
With smiling plenty, and fair prosperous days![1]

In the tragedies, this dialectic of the fall and redemption appears so evident that it becomes the very object of the plot. From *Romeo and Juliet* to *Coriolanus* a whole world is faced with a damnation that finally reveals itself for what it really is. There are some characters who renounce and give up right away: Claudius, Macbeth, Edmund of Gloucester... They admittedly do not err on the side of hope, or only slightly so. Never do any of them perceive their crime as the harbinger of peace; rather they seem convinced of its futility and commit it merely to fulfill the ritual law of sacrifice. There are others – Brutus, Hamlet, Othello, Lear, Anthony – who resort to crime only after a long and exhausting struggle, as if the world, thirsting for their blood, slowly forces them to the breaking point. Assassins or victims, they fall as a scapegoat to the mystery of a redemption which they do not fully understand. At the moment of death, it seems that the future is already leading them – as with Hero the monk – to the site of their transfiguration:

Come, lady, die to live... [2]

Thus for Shakespeare the evolution from comedy to tragedy is nothing more than the evolution from the possibility to the act, from the implicit to the explicit. Everything which remained veiled and unformulated in the comedies appears as the very core of reality in the tragedies. The veils have been stripped away: it is in the naked symbol that man must find and define himself. Here each word becomes incarnate, each thought is projected as an hallucination. The invisible suddenly demands to be seen, and delegates its ghosts and witches to summon the living. Even the

---

[1] *Richard III*, V, 4, 35–47.
[2] *Much Ado About Nothing*, IV, 1, 255.

most obscure wishes, the most deeply concealed perfidies will not escape the fatality of light:

> *Time shall unfold what plighted cunning hides;*
> *Who covers faults, at last shame them derides.*[1]

Paradoxically, the tragedies thus prove to be much less esoteric than the comedies, since their basic structure constantly coincides with the order of events. Whence their principal problem: the conflict between fate and free will. If Valentine and Bassanio seem to be unconsciously directed by secret influences, every influence henceforth must be classed as deterministic. There can be no illusion about the heroes' responsibility for their acts, for their liberty, as Spinoza would say, is nothing more than their ignorance of the causes which made them act. But as soon as these causes are formulated in their mind they are seized by an implacable lucidity which drives them to despair and madness. Life seems merely a farce to be played by everyone, and the world a giant stage upon which the game must go on to the bitter end:

> *I see the play so lies that I must bear a part.*
> *No remedy.*
>
> *Go play, boy, play; thy mother plays, and I*
> *Play too, but so disgrac'd a part, whose issue*
> *Will hiss me to my grave.*[2]

Thus the themes of these tragedies represent for the most part merely a monstrous degradation of the earlier themes. Antonio's melancholy in *The Merchant of Venice* darkens into that of Jaques in *As You Like It*, and in *Hamlet* attains pathological proportions. The clearing where the lovers drop down in *A Midsummer Night's Dream* thickens into that unhealthy forest where Timon of Athens insults the thieves and whores. The gay confusion that reigns in Ephesus changes into the rottenness in Denmark. The castle where Portia so regally receives her guests degenerates into the lair where Lady Macbeth plots the murder of Duncan. Proteus' jealousy of Valentine becomes the frightful hate that Edmund bears Edgar and Iago has for Othello; Jessica's revolt against

---

[1] *King Lear*, I, 1. 283–284.
[2] *The Winter's Tale*, IV, 3, 672–673; I, 2, 187–189.

Shylock is matched by the base ingratitude of Lear's daughters for their father. Even the characters' virtues are doomed to depravity. Macbeth's courage is engulfed by crime, Anthony's love degenerates to lust, and Coriolanus' honor to pride. And not only men, but the elements themselves are perverted, so that here everything degenerates, hastens towards an immense apocalypse. But through its own excesses evil finds its remission. Fortinbras' victory, Malcolm's coronation already herald the era of innocence. Conceived in terror and suffering, a whole world at last finds truth in the pardon and serenity of *The Tempest*.

Is it by chance that the fairy-plays which bring to a close these dismal tragedies revert to the symbol of resurrection that marked Shakespeare's early works? Already in *Romeo and Juliet* a girl in love ventured into the grave, there to await the hour of fond farewell. In *Much Ado About Nothing*, Hero feigned death till, exonerated of her alleged offenses, she could claim her wedding dress. Again, in *All's Well that Ends Well*, Helen returned from the other world to confound Bertram. And in *Measure for Measure* Claudio had reappeared before Isabella after she had been shown his head decapitated. And now in turn *Pericles* bears witness to the fact that '*death may usurp on nature many hours and yet the fire of life kindle again.*' In *Cymbeline*, Imogen awakes from the grave where her brothers had laid her just as Posthumus, thinking he had killed her, is on the verge of joining her. And *The Winter's Tale* teaches us how Hermione, with the magic help of music, was '*stolen from the dead*'...

> *O benefit of ill! now I find true*
> *That better is by evil still made better.*[1]

And it was indeed necessary for a Hamlet or a Lear to suffer to the limit of human endurance so that life might once again pronounce the word 'mercy'. This resurrection, the whole mystery of love, finds its ultimate expression in *The Tempest*. After the shipwreck, the fear, and estrangement, the guilty learn that their sins have been forgiven them. Near the sea, they once again discover the memory of the eternal, in Miranda the purity, as in Ariel the splendor of the angel at last triumphant over the beast. All regrets having been voiced, and with reason restored

---

[1] *Sonnet CXIX.*

to its rightful place, Prospero forgives and proclaims the coming of a brave new world at the end of the play. Thus the extraordinary Shakespearean drama ends with an apotheosis: on a distant isle, through the grace of a sage, the living hail the dawn of a golden age.

Texts

The dramatist is necessarily the enemy of the singular. The writer of memoirs and intimate diaries must look within himself for his material, but the author of drama is, on the contrary, forced to efface and forget himself, to project. Nothing lends itself more poorly to personal revelations than does this art in which a hundred different faces mask the author's own. Shakespeare tells us nothing about himself, but he tells us everything about man. Thus we would be doing him no injustice if we were to concern ourselves with his thought rather than with him as a person. In these pages we therefore propose to examine Shakespeare's work in an effort to determine exactly what he had to say on the following subjects: love, nature, history, evil, death, and poetry.

Love

For Orpheus' lute was strung with poets' sinews,
Whose golden touch could soften steel and stones,
Make tigers tame and huge leviathans
Forsake unsounded deeps to dance on sands.
After your dire-lamenting elegies,
Visit by night your lady's chamber-window
With some sweet consort: to their instruments
Tune a deploring dump; the night's dead silence
Will well become such sweet-complaining grievance.

The Two Gentlemen of Verona, III, 2, 78–86

*For to love means first to suffer, as Shakespeare must have learned
fairly early in life.*

To be in love, where scorn is bought with groans;
Coy looks with heart-sore sighs; one fading moment's mirth
With twenty watchful, weary, tedious nights:
If haply won, perhaps a hapless gain;
If lost, why then a grievous labour won:
However, but a folly bought with wit,
Or else a wit by folly vanquished.

Ibid., I, 1, 29–35

119

Whence the easily understandable suspicion of rational men:

I do much wonder that one man, seeing how much another man is a fool when he dedicates his behaviours to love, will, after he hath laughed at such shallow follies in others, become the argument of his own scorn by falling in love: and such a man is Claudio. I have known, when there was no music but the drum and fife; and now had he rather hear the tabor and the pipe: I have known, when he would have walked ten mile afoot to see a good armour; and now will he lie ten nights awake, carving the fashion of a new doublet. He was wont to speak plain and to the purpose, like an honest man and a soldier; and now he is turned orthographer; his words are a very fantastical banquet, just so many strange dishes. May I be so converted, and see with these eyes?

Much Ado About Nothing, II, 3, 7–24

Rather flout 'the wily breed of women':

Would God would serve the world so all the year! we'd find no fault with the tithe-woman if I were the parson. One in ten, quoth a'! An we might have a good woman born but for every blazing star, or at an earthquake, 'twould mend the lottery well.

All's Well That Ends Well, I, 3, 88–93

Unfortunately, these sarcasms are of little use against the unforeseen. As misfortune strikes man in the twinkling of an eye, so can passion and absurdity take hold of him with equal swiftness.

TRIANO. I pray, sir, tell me, is it possible
That love should of a sudden take such hold?
LUCENTIO. O Triano! till I found it to be true,
I never thought it possible or likely;
But see, while idly I stood looking on,
I found the effect of love in idleness;
And now in plainness do confess to thee,
That art to me as secret and as dear
As Anna to the Queen of Carthage was,
Triano, I burn, I pine, I perish, Triano,
If I achieve not this young modest girl.

The Taming of the Shrew, I, 1, 150–160

Love is thus this sudden flame, this violent intrusion of wonder:

ROMEO. What lady is that which doth enrich the hand

Of yonder knight?

SERV. I know not, sir.

ROMEO. O! she doth teach the torches to burn bright.
It seems she hangs upon the cheek of night
Like a rich jewel in an Ethiop's ear;
Beauty too rich for use, for earth too dear!
So shows a snowy dove trooping with crows,
As yonder lady oe'r her fellows shows.
The measure done, I'll watch her place of stand,
And, touching hers, make blessed my rude hand.
Did my heart love till now? forswear it, sight!
For I ne'er saw true beauty till this night.

Romeo and Juliet, 1, 5, 45–57

A scene from The Taming of the Shrew.

But scarcely has he been afflicted, when the lover sees proliferous signs of his sickness—obsession:

When I would pray and think, I think and pray
To several subjects: heaven hath my empty words,

121

Whilst my invention, hearing not my tongue,
Anchors on Isabel: heaven in my mouth,
As if I did but only chew his name,
And in my heart the strong and swelling evil
Of my conception.

Measure For Measure, II, 4, 1–7

extravagance:

> CLAUDIO. If he be not in love with some woman, there is no
> believing old signs: a' brushes his hat a mornings; what
> should that bode?
> DON PEDRO. Hath any man seen him at the barber's?
> CLAUDIO. No, but the barber's man hath been seen with him;
> and the old ornament of his cheek hath already stuffed
> tennis-balls.
> LEONATO. Indeed he looks younger than he did, by the loss
> of a beard.
> DON PEDRO. Nay, a' rubs himself with civet: can you smell
> him out by that?
> CLAUDIO. That's as much as to say the sweet youth's in love.
> *Much Ado About Nothing*, III, 2, 40–53

And from that moment on,

> Adieu, valour! rust, rapier! be still, drum! for your manager
> is in love; yea, he loveth. Assist me some extemporal god of
> rime, for I am sure I shall turn sonneter. Devise, wit; write,
> pen; for I am for whole volumes in folio.
> *Love's Labour's Lost*, I, 2, 190–195

*But what's the way to win a lady? Shakespeare is going to tell us
how by composing, in his poems and comedies, a veritable 'art of
loving.'*

> O learn to love; the lesson is but plain,
> And once made perfect, never lost again.
> *Venus And Adonis*, 407–408

Is one king? He has only to declare himself:

> Marry, if you would put me to verses, or to dance for your
> sake, Kate, why you undid me: for the one I have neither
> words nor measure, and for the other I have no strength in
> measure... If thou would have such a one, take me; and take
> me, take a soldier; take a soldier, take a king. And what

sayest thou then to my love? speak, my fair, and fairly, I
pray thee.

Henry V, V, 2, 136–176

Is one a soldier? He has only to tell about his campaigns:

Her father lov'd me; oft invited me;
Still question'd me the story of my life
From year to year, the battles, sieges, fortunes
That I have pass'd.
I ran it through, even from my boyish days
To the very moment that he bade me tell it...
This to hear
Would Desdemona seriously incline;
But still the house-affairs would draw her thence;
Which ever as she could with haste dispatch,
She'd come again, and with a greedy ear
Devour up my discourse...
She lov'd me for the dangers I had pass'd,
And I lov'd her that she did pity them.

Othello, I, 3, 128–168

Is one a greybeard? He has only to be generous:

> Win her with gifts, if she respect not words;
> Dumb jewels often in their silent kind
> More than quick words do move a woman's mind.
>
> *The Two Gentlemen of Verona*, III, 1, 89–91

And if ever her doors should remain closed, then scale a wall at night and hide in the shadows:

> JULIET. How cam'st thou thither, tell me, and wherefore?
> The orchard walls are high and hard to climb,
> And the place death, considering who thou art,
> If any of my kinsmen find thee here.
> ROMEO. With love's light wings did I o'erperch these walls;
> For stony limits cannot hold love out,
> And what love can do that dares love attempt;
> Therefore thy kinsmen are no stop to me.
> JULIET. If they do see thee they will murder thee...
> ROMEO. I have night's cloak to hide me from their eyes.
>
> *Romeo and Juliet*, II, 2, 62–75

Together with daring, verve and repartee are thus the seducer's surest arms:

> Flatter and praise, commend, extol their graces;
> Though ne'er so black, say they have angels' faces.
> That man that hath a tongue, I say, is no man,
> If with his tongue he cannot win a woman.
>
> *The Two Gentlemen of Verona*, III, 1, 102–105

If necessary, music can compensate for other shortcomings:

> LOVELL.   Ay, marry,
> There will be woe indeed, lords: the sly whoresons
> Have got a speeding trick to lay down ladies;
> A French song and a fiddle has no fellow.
> SANDS. The devil fiddle 'em!
>
> *Henry VIII*, I, 3, 39–42

Or dancing:

> SIR TOBY. What is thy excellence in a galliard, knight?
> SIR ANDREW. Faith, I can cut a caper.
> SIR TOBY. And I can cut the mutton to't.
> SIR ANDREW. And I think I have the back-trick simply as
> strong as any man in Illyria.

SIR TOBY. Wherefore are these things hid? wherefore have these gifts a curtain before 'em? are they like to take dust, like Mistress Mall's picture? why dost thou not go to church in a galliard, and come home in a coranto? My very walk should be a jig: I would not so much as make water but in a sink-a-pace. What dost thou mean? is it a world to hide virtues in? I did think, by the excellent constitution of thy leg, it was formed under the star of a galliard.

Twelfth Night, I, 3, 129–144

Such are the familiar ruses, young ladies, by which

Virginity being blown down, man will quicklier be blown up: marry in blowing him down again, with the breach yourselves made, you lose your city. It is not politic in the commonwealth of nature to preserve virginity. Loss of virginity is rational increase...

All's Well That Ends Well, I, 1, 136–141

For the mission of the living is to grow and multiply.

Nature carved thee for her seal, and meant thereby
Thou shouldst print more, nor let that copy die.

Sonnet XI

With these strong words, Shakespeare leaves the married couple to live happily ever after. But order and happiness do not always prevail:

Ay me! for aught that ever I could read,
Could ever hear by tale or history,
The course of true love never did run smooth;
But, either it was different in blood, –

A Midsummer Night's Dream, I, 1, 132–135

or an irascible father:

...mistress minion, you
Thank me no thankings, nor proud me no prouds,
But fettle your fine joints 'gainst Thursday next,
To go with Paris to Saint Peter's church,
Or I will drag thee on a hurdle thither.
Out, you green-sickness carrion! out, you baggage!
You tallow face!

Romeo and Juliet, III, 5, 152–158

And the lovers' farewells already bespeak death:

> JULIET. O God! I have an ill-divining soul:
>   Methinks I see thee, now thou art so low,
>   As one dead in the bottom of a tomb:
>   Either my eyesight fails, or thou look'st pale.
> ROMEO. And trust me, love, in my eye so do you:
>   Dry sorrow drinks our blood. Adieu! adieu!

Ibid:, III, 5, 54–59

Thus love has many dangers. But these worldly obstacles are not the most serious, for passion itself contains the most bitter seed of all, doubt:

> As love is full of unbefitting strains;
> All wanton as a child, skipping and vain;
> Form'd by the eye, and, therefore, like the eye,
> Full of stray shapes, of habits and of forms,
> Varying in subjects, as the eye doth roll
> To every varied object in his glance.

Love's Labour's Lost, V, 2, 768–773

Even the purest union is not free of this secret doubt, this fear of inconstancy:

> ROMEO. Lady, by yonder blessed moon I swear
>   That tips with silver all these fruit-tree tops, –
> JULIET. O! swear not by the moon, the inconstant moon,
>   That monthly changes in her circles orb,
>   Lest that thy love prove likewise variable.

Romeo and Juliet, II, 2, 107–111

Inconstancy: therein lies the source of our faults and despair:

> That it should come to this!
> But two months dead: nay, not so much, not two:
> So excellent a king; that was, to this,
> Hyperion to a satyr; so loving to my mother
> That he might not beteem the winds of heaven
> Visit her face too roughly. Heaven and earth!
> Must I remember? why, she would hang on him,
> As if increase of appetite had grown
> By what it fed on; and yet, within a month,
> Let me not think on't: Frailty, thy name is woman!
> A little month; or ere those shoes were old
> With which she follow'd my poor father's body,

Like Niobe, all tears; why she, even she, –
O God! a beast, that wants discourse of reason,
Would have mourn'd longer, – married with mine uncle,
My father's brother, but no more like my father
Than I to Hercules: within a month,
Ere yet the salt of most unrighteous tears
Had left the flushing in her galled eyes,
She married. O! most wicked speed, to post
With such dexterity to incestuous sheets.
It is not nor it cannot come to good;
But break, my heart, for I must hold my tongue!

Hamlet, I, 2, 137–159

*Unhappily, this inconstancy is the mark of human nature. We
cannot remain as we are:*

> The present pleasure,
> By revolution lowering, does become
> The opposite of itself.

Anthony and Cleopatra, I, 2, 133–135

> Women are angels, wooing:
> Things won are done; joy's soul lies in the doing.

Troilus and Cressida, I, 2, 310–311

Thus a tragic distance separates us:

HERMIA. The more I hate, the more he follows me.
HELEN. The more I love, the more he hateth me.

A Midsummer Night's Dream, I, 1, 198–199

a distance matched only by that which separates fact from ideal:

This is the monstruosity in love, lady,
that the will is infinite, and the execution
confined; that the desire is boundless,
and the act a slave to limit.

Troilus and Cressida, III, 2, 85–88

How then can this lie be taken seriously?

It is merely a lust of the blood and a permission of the will.

Othello, I, 3, 339–340

Love is merely a madness, and, I tell you, deserves as well a
dark house and a whip as madmen do.

As You Like It, III, 2, 426–428

Hence the constant danger of cuckoldry, which Shakespeare, like Rabelais, often chooses to mock:

> There have been,
> Or I am much deceiv'd, cuckolds ere now;
> And many a man there is even at this present
> Now, while I speak this, holds his wife by the arm,
> That little thinks she has been sluic'd in's absence.
>
> *The Winter's Tale*, I, 2, 190–194

All these aberrations and base deeds make misogyny especially bitter:

> Behold yond simpering dame,
> Whose face between her forks presageth snow;
> That minces virtue, and does shake the head
> To hear of pleasure's name;
> The fitchew nor the soil'd horse goes to't
> With a more riotous appetite.
> Down from the waist they are Centaurs,
> Though women all above:
> But to the girdle do the gods inherit,
> Beneath is all the fiends':
> There's hell, there's darkness, there is the sulphurous pit,
> Burning, scalding, stench, consumption; fie, fie,
> fie! pah, pah! Give me an ounce of civet, good
> apothecary, to sweeten my imagination: there's money for thee.
>
> *King Lear*, IV, 6, 121–135

> Is there no way for men to be, but women
> Must be half-workers? We are all bastards; all,
> And the most venerable man which I
> Did call my father was I know not where
> When I was stamp'd...
>   Could I find out
> The woman's part in me! For there's no motion
> That tends to vice in man but I affirm
> It is the woman's part; be it lying, note it,
> The woman's; flattering, hers; deceiving, hers;
> Lust and rank thoughts, hers, hers; revenges, hers;
> Ambitions, covetings, change of prides, disdain,
> Nice longing, slanders, mutability,
> All faults that man may name, nay, that hell knows,
> Why, hers, in part, or all; but rather, all.
>
> *Cymbeline*, II, 5, 1–28

But it is significant that these imprecations are the result of mis-understandings, and apply only to the ill-starred excesses of passion. True love, on the contrary, requires giving oneself completely and unreservedly:

JULIET. What satisfaction canst thou have tonight?
ROMEO. The exchange of thy love's faithful vow for mine.
JULIET. I gave thee mine before thou didst request it;
    And yet I would it were to give again.
ROMEO. Wouldst thou withdraw it? for what purpose love?
JULIET. But to be frank, and give it thee again.
    And yet I wish but for the thing I have:
    My bounty is as boundless as the sea,
    My love as deep; the more I give to thee,
    The more I have, for both are infinite.
Romeo and Juliet, II, 2, 126–135

Thus love which is freely given and faithfully kept to inspires poetry, like a state of grace:

Admir'd Miranda!
Indeed, the top of admiration; worth
What's dearest to the world!...
The Tempest, III, 1, 37–39

But it is time to clarify Shakespeare's use of this language. Under the guise of glorifying a certain heroine, the poet is urging us to adore this 'celestial lover' whose praises the troubadours also sang, and these declarations here contain a second, metaphysical meaning:

It is thyself, mine own self's better part;
Mine eye's clear eye, my dear heart's dearer heart;
My food, my fortune, and my sweet hope's aim,
My sole earth's heaven, and my heaven's claim.
The Comedy of Errors, III, 2, 61–64

It is my soul that calls upon my name:
How silver-sweet sound lovers' tongues by night,
Like softest music to attending ears!
Romeo and Juliet, II, 2, 164–166

So love, like an initiation, introduces us to the 'true science,' the 'gaya scienza'

Can you still dream and pore and thereon look?
For when would you, my lord, or you, or you,

Have found the ground of study's excellence
Without the beauty of a woman's face?

Love's Labour's Lost, IV, 3, 298–301

And the poet at last reveals his secret:
From women's eyes this doctrine I derive:
They sparkle still the right Promethean fire;
They are the books, the arts, the academes,
That show, contain and nourish all the world.

Ibid. IV, 3, 350–353

and his advice:
Be prodigal: the lamp that burns by night
Dries up his oil to lend the world his light.

Venus and Adonis, 755–756

Nature

Thus sometimes hath the brightest day a cloud;
And after summer evermore succeeds
Barren in winter, with his wrathful nipping cold:
So cares and joys abound as seasons fleet.

Henry VI, Part II, II, 4, 1–4

Men's fate is not a solitary matter, for man is part of the universal order of things. And it is this very fact which allows the seer to pretend that:

In nature's infinite book of secrecy
A little I can read.

Anthony and Cleopatra, I, 2, 10–11

and the thief to confess:

For we that take purses go by the moon and the seven stars, and not by Phoebus, he, 'that wandering knight so fair.' ...Marry, then, sweet wag, when thou art king, let not us that are squires of the night's body be called thieves of the day's beauty: let us be Diana's foresters, gentlemen of the shade, minions of the moon; and let men say, we be men of good government, being governed as the sea is, by our noble and chaste mistress the moon, under whose countenance we steal.

Henry IV, Part I, I, 2, 15–33

Thus we should be convinced that our life is in constant contact with creation, and the problem of solitude is immediately resolved:

It is the stars,
The stars above us, govern our conditions.

King Lear, IV, 3, 34–35

a condition which applies to nations as well:

Mars his true moving, even as in the heavens,
So in the earth, to this day is not known.
Late did he shine upon the English side;
Now we are the victors; upon us he smiles.

Henry VI, Part I, I, 2, 1–4

The first principle of alchemy – that which is above is as that which is below – is beautifully illustrated here. Even as with man, so with the universe: the same laws govern both.

The heavens themselves, the planets, and this centre
Observe degree, priority, and place,
Insisture, course, proportion, season, form,
Office, and custom, in all line of order:
And therefore is the glorious planet Sol
In noble eminence enthron'd and spher'd
Amidst the other; whose med'cinable eye
Corrects the ill aspects of planets evil,
And posts, like the commandments of a king,
Sans check, to good and bad: but when the planets
In evil mixture to disorder wander,
What plagues, and what portents, what mutiny,
What raging of the sea, shaking of earth,
Commotion in the winds, frights, changes, horrors,
Divert and crack, rend and deracinate
The unity and married calm of states
Quite from their fixure! O! when degree is shak'd,
Which is the ladder to all high designs,
The enterprise is sick. How could communities,
Degrees in schools, and brotherhood in cities,
Peaceful commerce from dividable shores,
The primogenitive and due of birth,
Prerogative of age, crowns, sceptres, laurels,
But by degree, stand in authentic place?
Take but degree away, untune that string,
And, hark! what discord follows; each thing meets
In mere oppugnancy; the bounded waters

Should lift their bosoms higher than the shores,
And make a sop of all this solid globe:
Strength should be lord of imbecility,
And the rude son should strike his father dead:
Force should be right; or, rather, right and wrong –
Between whose endless jar justice resides –
Should lose their names, and so should justice too.
Then every thing includes itself in power,
Power into will, will into appetite;
And appetite, a universal wolf,
So doubly seconded with will and power,
Must make perforce a universal prey,
And last eat up himself.

Troilus and Cressida, I, 3, 85–124

In this important passage we find described both the system of the Elizabethan world and the metamorphoses which were to mark the Shakespearean concept of nature: from order to disorder, from chaos to serenity. Beginning with an idyllic feeling of the landscape, the poet first tries his wings with those pleasant pastorals that were so much admired by his contemporaries:

When daisies pied and violets blue
And lady-smocks all silver-white
And cuckoo-buds of yellow hue
Do paint the meadows with delight,
The cuckoo then, on every tree,
Mocks married men, for thus sings he,
        Cuckoo;
Cuckoo, cuckoo: O, word of fear,
Unpleasing to a married ear!

Love's Labour's Lost, V, 2, 902–910

and expounds the naive moral they imply:

Now, my co-mates and brothers in exile,
Hath not old custom made this life more sweet
Than that of painted pomp? Are not these woods
More free from peril than the envious court?
Here feel we but the penalty of Adam,
The seasons' difference; as, the icy fang
And churlish chiding of the winter's wind,
Which, when it bites and blows upon my body,
Even till I shrink with cold, I smile and say
'This is no flattery: these are counsellors

That feelingly persuade me what I am.'
Sweet are the uses of adversity,
Which like the toad, ugly and venomous,
Wears yet a precious jewel in his head;
And this our life exempt from public haunt
Finds tongues in trees, books in the running brooks,
Sermons in stones, and good in every thing.
I would not change it.

As You Like It, II, 1, 1–18

So nature's innocence is contrasted to the cities' corruption. Un-
happily, it will not play this role for very long. For it suffices that
a certain wind begins to blow and...
For do but stand upon the foaming shore,
The chidden billow seems to pelt the clouds;
The wind-shak'd surge, with high and monstrous mane,
Seems to cast water on the burning bear
And quench the guards of the ever-fixed pole.

Othello, II, 1, 11–15

Geography itself partakes of its terrors, as is illustrated by the cliffs
of Dover:
How fearful and dizzy 'tis to cast one's eyes so low!
The crows and choughs that wing the midway air
Show scarce so gross as beetles; half way down
Hangs one that gathers samphire, dreadful trade!
Methinks he seems no bigger than his head.
The fishermen that walk upon the beach
Appear like mice, and yond tall anchoring bark
Diminished to her cock, her cock a buoy
Almost too small for sight. The murmuring surge,
That on the unnumber'd idle pebbles chafes,
Cannot be heard so high. I'll look no more,
Lest my brain turn, and the deficient sight
Topple down headlong.

King Lear, IV, 6, 12–25

And now this nature, which is fundamentally good, begins to assume
another, deadly aspect:
THIRD FISHERMAN. Master, I marvel how the fishes live in the
sea.
FIRST FISHERMAN. Why, as men do a-land; the great ones eat
up the little ones. *Pericles*, II, 1, 29–32

So it is not surprising that this side of nature is in tune with our misfortunes, as its pleasant side is in tune with our pleasures.

These late eclipses in the sun and moon portend no good to us: though the wisdom of nature can reason it thus and thus, yet nature finds itself scourged by the sequent effects. Love cools, friendship falls off, brothers divide: in cities, mutinies; in countries, discord; in palaces, treason; and the bond cracked between son and father.

King Lear, I, 2, 115–122

And nature is prophetic: endowed with a monstrous prescience, it seems forewarned of coming disasters.

In the most high and palmy state of Rome,
A little ere the mightiest Julius fell,
The graves stood tenantless and the sheeted dead
Did squeak and gibber in the Roman streets;
As stars with trains of fire and dews of blood,
Disasters in the sun; and the moist star
Upon whose influence Neptune's empire stands
Was sick almost to doomsday with eclipse.

Hamlet, I, 1, 113–120

Henceforth nature's only mission will be to prepare the way for catastrophes.

The night has been unruly: where we lay,
Our chimneys were blown down; and, as they say,
Lamenting heard i' the air; strange screams of death,
And prophesying with accents terrible
Of dire combustion and confus'd events
New hatch'd to the woeful time. The obscure bird
Clamour'd the livelong night: some say the earth
Was feverous and did shake.

Macbeth, II, 3, 59–67

As for the heroes, they are so convinced of this participation that their fall brings on the Apocalypse.

My wife! my wife! what wife? I have no wife:
O insupportable! O heavy hour!
Methinks it should be now a high eclipse
Of sun and moon, and that the afflicted globe
Should yawn at alteration.

Othello, V, 2, 96–100

One step further and we can make nature responsible for our crimes:

    It is the very error of the moon;
    She comes more near the earth than she was wont,
    And makes men mad.

Ibid., V, 2, 107–108

Thus nature is transformed from a herald of evil to evil itself, and we move into the darkest phase of Shakespeare's work. The most vile evil rises from its depths to cover men like a thick shroud of night.

    The gaudy, blabbing, and remorseful day

Lear: a portrait of madness.

Is crept into the bosom of the sea,
And now loud-howling wolves arouse the jades
That drag the tragic melancholy night;
Who with their drowsy, slow, and flagging wings
Clip dead men's graves, and from their misty jaws
Breathe foul contagious darkness in the air.

Henry VI, Part II, IV, 1, 1–7

*The satanic power of the elements overwhelms man. In such a
situation he has no other recourse than to ride out the storm:*

Wind, rain, and thunder, remember, earthly man
Is but a substance that must yield to you;
And I, as fits my nature, do obey you.

Pericles, II, 1, 2–4

or to rage with the raging storm:

Blow, winds, and crack your cheeks! rage! blow!
You cataracts and hurricanoes, spout
Till you have drench'd our steeples, drown'd the cocks!
You sulphurous and thought-executing fires,
Vaunt-couriers to oak-cleaving thunderbolts,
Singe my white head! And thou, all-shaking thunder,
Strike flat the thick rotundity o' the world!
Crack nature's moulds, all germens spill at once
That make ingrateful man!

King Lear, III, 2, 1–9

*But in lending his support to chaos, man loses his last safeguard:
reason.*

Contending with the fretful elements;
Bids the wind blow the earth into the sea,
Or swell the curled waters 'bove the main,
That things might change or cease; tears his white hair,
Which the impetuous blasts, with eyeless rage,
Catch in their fury, and make nothing of;
Strives in his little world of man to out-scorn
The to-and-fro conflicting wind and rain.
This night, wherein the cub-drawn bear would couch,
The lion and the belly-pinched wolf
Keep their fur dry, unbonneted he runs,
And bids what will take all.

Ibid., III, 1, 4–14

According to Shakespeare, however, madness is often the way to salvation. As Antaeus' strength was renewed each time he touched the earth, so man, in losing himself in the cosmos, finds innocence, the attributes of a god.

I dream'd there was an Emperor Anthony...
His face was as the heavens, and therein stuck
A sun and moon, which kept their course, and lighted
The little O, the earth...
His legs bestrid the ocean; his rear'd arm
Crested the world; his voice was propertied
As all the tuned spheres, and that to friends;
But when he meant to quail and shake the orb,
He was as rattling thunder. For his bounty,
There was no winter in't, an autumn 'twas
That grew the more by reaping; his delights
Were dolphin-like, they show'd his back above
The element they liv'd in; in his livery
Walk'd crowns and crownets, realms and islands were
As plates dropp'd from his pocket.

Anthony and Cleopatra, V, 2, 76–92

Similarly, nature can only recover its former state by repairing the wrongs it has engendered. Once the criminals' accomplice, its role is now to restrain them or blot them out.

Blood will have blood;
Stones have been known to move and trees to speak;
Augurs and understood relations have
By maggot-pies and cloughs and rooks brought forth
The secret'st man of blood.

Macbeth, III, 4, 122–126

O, it is monstrous! monstrous!
Methought the billows spoke and told me of it;
The winds did sing it to me; and the thunder,
That deep and dreadful organ-pipe, pronounc'd
The name of Prosper: it did bass my trespass.

The Tempest, III, 3, 95–99

And the long night of tragedy finally ends.

I have heard,
The cock, that is the trumpet to the morn,
Doth with his lofty and shrill-sounding throat
Awake the god of day: and at his warning,

Whether in sea of fire, in earth or air,
The extravagant and erring spirit hies
To his confine.

Hamlet, I, 1, 149–155

As soon as evil is consummated, all the signs are reversed.
No natural exhalation in the sky,
No scope of nature, no distemper'd day,
No common wind, no customed event,
But they will pluck away his natural cause
And call them meteors, prodigies, and signs,
Abortives, presages, and tongues of heaven,
Plainly denouncing vengeance upon John.

King John, III, 4, 153–159

And as nature finds peace again,
If by your art, my dearest father, you have
Put the wild waters in this roar, allay them.

The Tempest, I, 2, 1–2

so man recovers his sense of responsibility:
This is the excellent foppery of the world, that, when we are
sick in fortune, – often the surfeit of our own behaviour, – we
make guilty of our disasters the sun, the moon, and the stars;
as if we were villians by necessity, fools by heavenly compul-
sion, knaves, thieves, and treachers by spherical predominance,
drunkards, liars, and adulterers by an enforced obedience of
planetary influence; and all that we are evil in, by a divine
thrusting on: an admirable evasion of whoremaster man, to
lay his goatish disposition to the charge of a star! My father
compounded with my mother under the dragon's tail, and
my nativity was under *ursa major;* so that it follows I am
rough and lecherous. 'Sfoot! I should have been that I am
had the maidenliest star in the firmament twinkled on my
bastardizing.

King Lear, I, 2, 132–149

Balance within, balance without. With the hurricanes calmed,
everything once again assumes the aspect of the miraculous:
Tempests themselves, high seas, and howling winds
The gutter'd rocks, and congregated sands,
Traitors ensteep'd to clog the guiltless keel,
As having sense of beauty, do omit

Their mortal natures, letting go safely by
The divine Desdemona.

Othello, II, 1, 68–73

*But the reason for this final metamorphosis perhaps stems from the
return of the poet to the scene of his early years. For as he grew
older he left the city and returned to these woods and fields and
meadows, to everything that summer wears to receive the prodigal
poet:*

Why should you want? Behold, the earth hath roots;
Within this mile break forth a hundred springs;
The oaks bear mast, the briers scarlet hips;
The bounteous housewife, nature, on each bush
Lays her full mess before you.

Timon of Athens, IV, 3, 423–427

And, as in the Pastoral Symphony, *Shakespeare sings the praises
of work and time, of the peace and immense fertility of the earth,
in a final and beautiful hymn:*

Ceres, most bounteous lady, thy rich leas
Of wheat, rye, barley, vetches, oats, and peas;
Thy turfy mountains, where live nibbling sheep,
And flat meads thatch'd with stover, them to keep;
Thy banks with pioned and twilled brims,
Which spongy April at thy hest betrims,
To make cold nymphs chaste crowns; and thy broom groves,
Whose shadow the dismissed bachelor loves,
Being lass-lorn; thy pole-clipt vineyard;
And thy sea-marge, sterile and rocky-hard,
Where thou thyself dost air: the queen o' the sky,
Whose watery arch and messenger am I,
Bids thee leave these; and with her sovereign grace,
Here on this grass-plot, in this very place,
To come and sport; her peacocks fly amain:
Approach, rich Ceres, her to entertain.

The Tempest, IV, 1, 60–75

History

These metamorphoses that Shakespeare reveals in man as well as nature result in a whole dialectic of order and disorder in his work. But is there any reality to which this philosophy could be better suited than to society, or to politics and history? Here the poet at last discovered a lasting, natural tragedy, a vivid subject fully worthy of his aspirations:

O! for a Muse of fire, that would ascend
The brightest heaven of invention;
A kingdom for a stage, princes to act
And monarchs to behold the swelling scene.

Henry V, Chorus preceding Act I

But, on the point of invoking them, he is careful to avoid any misunderstanding:

Of government the properties to unfold,
Would seem in me to affect speech and discourse,
Since I am put to know that your own science
Exceeds, in that, the lists of all advice
My strength can give you.

Measure for Measure, I, 1, 3–7

Shakespeare is not concerned with theory. The role of the theatre is to portray rather than to codify history, and unfortunately his judgment begins with a condemnation, for here,

One fire drives out one fire; one nail, one nail;
Rights by rights falter, strengths by strengths do fail.

Coriolanus, IV, 7, 54–55

141

The abuse of greatness is when it disjoins
Remorse from power.

Julius Caesar, II, 1, 18–19

Since these dissensions lead man to an endless struggle against others and against himself, the moralist is obliged to denounce them as useless:

HAMLET. What have you, my good friends, deserved at the hands of Fortune, that she sends you to prison hither?

GUILDENSTERN. Prison, my Lord!

HAMLET. Denmark's a prison.

ROSENCRANTZ. Then is the world one.

HAMLET. A goodly one; in which there are many confines, wards, and dungeons, Denmark being one o' the worst.

ROSENCRANTZ. We think not so, my lord.

HAMLET. Why, then, 'tis none to you; for there is nothing either good or bad, but thinking makes it so: to me it is a prison.

ROSENCRANTZ. Why, then your ambition makes it one; 'tis too narrow for your mind.

HAMLET. O God! I could be bounded in a nutshell, and count myself a king of infinite space, were it not that I have bad dreams.

GUILDENSTERN. Which dreams, indeed, are ambitions, for the very substance of the ambitious is merely the shadow of a dream.

HAMLET. A dream itself is but a shadow.

ROSENCRANTZ. Truly, and I hold ambition of so airy and light a quality that it is but a shadow's shadow.

HAMLET. Then are our beggars bodies, and our monarchs and outstretched heroes the beggars' shadows.

Hamlet, II, 2, 249–276

Ambition's most common goal, wealth, is also denounced by the poet:

Gold! yellow, glittering precious gold!...
Thus much of this will make black white, foul fair,
Wrong right, base noble, old young, coward valiant...
This yellow slave
Will knit and break religions: bless the accurs'd;
Make the hoar leprosy ador'd; place thieves,
And give them title, knee, and approbation,
With senators on the bench; this is it

Eug. Delacroix
1843.

Hamlet: *the scene with the ghost.*

That makes the wappen'd widow wed again;
She, whom the spital-house and ulcerous sores
Would cast the gorge at, this embalms and spices
To the April day again. Come, damned earth,
Thou common whore of mankind, that putt'st odds
Among the rout of nations, I will make thee
Do thy right nature.

Timon of Athens, IV, 3, 26–44

But in history ambition is otherwise significant, for it aims not so much at wealth as at domination:

Thou art, if thou dar'st be, the earthly Jove:
Whate'er the ocean pales, or sky inclips,
Is thine, if thou wilt ha't.

Anthony and Cleopatra, II, 7, 74–76

This philosophy prevails in all classes of society, for while in high places cynicism is rife . . .

Learn this, brother,
We live not to be grip'd by meaner persons.

Henry VIII, II, 2, 135–136

the people also teach us that a resounding victory is worth more than any precept:

FIRST CITIZEN. Heralds, from off our towers we might behold
The first to last, the onset and retire
Of both your armies; whose equality
By our best eyes cannot be censured:
Blood hath brought blood, and blows have answer'd blows;
Strength match'd with strength, and power confronted
Both are alike; and both alike we like   [power:
One must prove greatest, while they weigh so even,
We hold our town for neither, yet for both.

King John, II, 1, 325–333

This being the case, we can see why the job of king is a difficult one and why those who hold it look upon rest as paradise:

How many thousand of my poorest subjects
Are at this hour asleep! O sleep! O gentle sleep!
Nature's soft nurse, how have I frighted thee,
That thou no more wilt weigh my eyelids down
And steep my senses in forgetfulness?
Why rather, sleep, liest thou in smoky cribs,
Upon uneasy pallets stretching thee,

And hush'd with buzzing night-flies to thy slumber,
Than in the perfum'd chambers of the great,
Under the canopies of costly state,
And lull'd with sound of sweetest melody?
O thou dull god! why liest thou with the vile
In loathsome beds, and leav'st the kingly couch
A watch-case or a common 'larum bell.

Henry IV, Part 2, III, 1, 4–17

*Yet the man who looks so desperately for peace can also achieve all
the world has to offer, and cry:*
The skies are painted with unnumber'd sparks,
They are all fire and every one doth shine,
But there's but one in all doth hold his place:
So, in the world; 'tis furnish'd well with men,
And men are flesh and blood, and apprehensive;
Yet in the number I do know but one
That unassailable holds on his rank,
Unshak'd of motion: and that I am he.

Julius Caesar, III, 1, 63–70

*What makes royalty so attractive is precisely this sacral function
that makes man an earthly god:*
Dear earth, I do salute thee with my hand,
Though rebels wound thee with their horses' hoofs:
As a long-parted mother with her child
Plays fondly with her tears and smiles in meeting,
So, weeping, smiling, greet I thee, my earth,
And do thee favour with my royal hands.
Feed not thy sovereign's foe, my gentle earth,
Nor with thy sweets comfort his ravenous sense;
But let thy spiders, that suck up thy venom
And heavy-gaited toads lie in their way,
Doing annoyance to the treacherous feet
Which with usurping steps do trample thee.
Yield stinging nettles to mine enemies;
And when they from thy bosom pluck a flower,
Guard it, I pray thee, with a lurking adder
Whose double tongue may with a mortal touch
Throw death upon thy sovereign's enemies.
Mock not my senseless conjuration, lords:
This earth shall have a feeling and these stones

Prove armed soldiers, ere her native king
Shall falter under foul rebellion's arms.

Richard II, III, 2, 6–26

Moreover, as the sun is sovereign of the universe, every monarch is its symbol. This well-known theme implies the cosmic notion of character which Shakespeare was to use with such striking effect:

Discomfortable cousin! Know'st thou not
That when the searching eye of heaven is hid
Behind the globe, and lights the lower world,
Then thieves and robbers range abroad unseen,
In murders and in outrage bloody here;
But when, from under this terrestrial ball
He fires the proud tops of the eastern pines
And darts his light through every guilty hole,
Then murders, treasons, and detested sins,
The cloak of night being pluck'd from off their backs,
Stand bare and naked, trembling at themselves?
So when this thief, this traitor, Bolingbroke,
Who all this while hath revell'd in the night
Whilst we were wandering with the antipodes,
Shall see us rising in our throne, the east,
His treasons will sit blushing in his face,

Not able to endure the sight of day,
But self-affrighted tremble at his sin.
Not all the water in the rough rude sea
Can wash the balm from an anointed king.

Ibid., III, 2, 35–55

If royalty is modeled on divine order, any attempt against it will provoke the worst catastrophes. As in the tragedies, nature will arm itself to make the guilty pay for this sacrilege.

O! pardon me, thou bleeding piece of earth,
That I am meek and gentle with these butchers;
Thou art the ruins of the noblest man
That ever lived in the tide of times.
Woe to the hand that shed this costly blood!
Over thy wounds now do I prophesy,
Which like dumb mouths do ope their ruby lips,
To beg the voice and utterance of my tongue,
A curse shall light upon the limbs of men;
Domestic fury and fierce civil strife
Shall cumber all the parts of Italy;
Blood and destruction shall be so in use,
And dreadful objects so familiar,
That mothers shall but smile when they behold
Their infants quarter'd with the hands of war;
All pity chok'd with custom of fell deeds:
And Caesar's spirit, ranging for revenge,
With Ate by his side come hot from hell,
Shall in these confines with a monarch's voice
Cry 'Havoc!' and let slip the dogs of war;
That this foul deed shall smell above the earth
With carrion men, groaning for burial.

Julius Caesar, III, 1, 254–275

Thus Shakespeare is right in saying:

The cease of majesty
Dies not alone, but, like a gulf doth draw
What's near it with it.

Hamlet, III, 3, 15–17

But such is the fatality of history that this majesty finds itself constantly threatened.

O! then that we could come by Caesar's spirit,
And not dismember Caesar. But, alas!

147

Caesar must bleed for it.

Julius Caesar, II, 1, 169–171

The most obvious enemies of this order are naturally its victims, the oppressed:
> The blunt monster with uncounted heads,
> The still-discordant wavering multitude.

Henry IV, Part 2, Induction, 18–19

We are accounted poor citizens, the patricians good. What authority surfeits on would relieve us. If they would yield us but the superfluity, while it were wholesome, we might guess they relieved us humanely; but they think we are too dear: the leanness that afflicts us, the object of our misery, is as an inventory to particularise their abundance; our sufferance is a gain to them. Let us revenge this with our pikes, ere we become rakes: for the gods know I speak this in hunger for bread, not in thirst for revenge.

Coriolanus, I, 1, 15–26

But rebellion gives rise to even greater discord and offers tyranny as its remedy. Plato has already discussed this point in his Republic, *and Shakespeare formulates it again here:*
> LUCIO. Why, how now, Claudio! whence comes this restraint?
> CLAUDIO. From too much liberty, my Lucio, liberty:
> As surfeit is the father of much fast
> So every scope by the immoderate use
> Turns to restraint. Our natures do pursue –
> Like rats that ravin down their proper bane, –
> A thirsty evil, and when we drink we die.

Measure For Measure, I, 2, 133–139

In such circumstances, the most radical method of nipping rebellions in the bud is to send the malcontents to the front lines:
> MESSENGER. The news is, sir, the Volsces are in arms.
> MARCIUS. I am glad on't; then we shall ha' means to vent
> Our musty superfluity.

Coriolanus, I, 1, 230–232

Two types of causes: rivalry among the mighty and the claims of the humble – or, to employ more modern terminology, the 'will to power' and the 'class struggle' – converge to explain the essence of history: war.
> Now all the youth of England are on fire,

And silken dalliance in the wardrobe lies;
Now thrive the armourers, and honour's thought
Reigns solely in the breast of every man:
They sell the pasture now to buy the horse,
Following the mirror of all Christian kings,
With winged heels, as English Mercuries.
For now sits Expectation in the air
And hides a sword from hilts unto the point
With crowns imperial, crowns and coronets,
Promis'd to Harry and his followers.

Henry V, II, Prologue, 1–11

*To describe war, Shakespeare had to resort to the most powerful
language at his command:*

How yet resolves the governor of the town?
This is the latest parle we will admit:
Therefore to our best mercy give yourselves;
Or like to men proud of destruction
Defy us to our worst: for, as I am a soldier, –
A name that in my thoughts, becomes me best, –
If I begin the battery once again,
I will not leave the half-achieved Harfleur
Till in her ashes she lie buried.
The gates of mercy shall be all shut up,
And the flesh'd soldier, rough and hard of heart,
In liberty of bloody hand shall range
With conscience wide as hell, mowing like grass
Your fresh-fair virgins and your flowering infants...
             Therefore, you men of Harfleur,
Take pity on your town and of your people,
Whiles yet my soldiers are in my command;
Whiles yet the cool and temperate wind of grace
O'erblows the filthy and contagious clouds
Of heady murder, spoil and villany.
If not, why, in a moment, look to see
The blind and bloody soldier with foul hand
Defile the locks of your shrill-shrieking daughters;
Your fathers taken by the silver beards,
And their most reverend heads dash'd to the walls;
Your naked infants spitted upon pikes,
Whiles the mad mothers with their howls confus'd
Do break the clouds, as did the wives of Jewry

At Herod's bloody-hunting slaughtermen.

Ibid., III, 3, 1–41

*By its very nature, however, the scourge carries within it the seeds
of its own destruction:*
> Swear against objects;
> Put armour on thine ears and on thine eyes,
> Whose proof nor yells of mothers, maids, nor babes,
> Nor sight of priests in holy vestments bleeding,
> Shall pierce a jot....
> Make large confusion; and thy fury spent,
> Confounded be thyself!

Timon of Athens, IV, 3, 123–129

*Those who live by the sword die by the sword. An immutable
fatality soon piles defeat upon defeat, till they are crushed.*
> FIRST MESSENGER. My gracious sovereign, now in Devonshire,
> As I by friends am well advertised,
> Sir Edward Courtney, and the haughty prelate,
> Bishop of Exeter, his brother there,
> With many moe confederates are in arms.
> SECOND MESSENGER. In Kent, my liege, the Guildfords are in
> And every hour more competitors   [arms;
> Flock to the rebels, and their power grows strong.
> THIRD MESSENGER. My lord, the army of great Buckingham –
> KING RICHARD. Out on ye, owls! nothing but songs of death?

Richard III, IV, 4, 499–508

*For everything in this world is subject to that fortune which Shakes-
peare, like the poets of the Middle Ages, likened to a wheel.*
> We, at the height, are ready to decline.

Julius Caesar, IV, 3, 216

> Nay, then, farewell!
> I have touch'd the highest point of all my greatness;
> And from that full meridian of my glory,
> I haste now to my setting: I shall fall
> Like a bright exhalation in the evening,
> And no man see me more.

Henry VIII, III, 2, 223–228

A good opportunity to think about the vanity of glory:
> O mighty Caesar! dost thou lie so low?
> Are all thy conquests, glories, triumphs, spoils,

Shrunk to this little measure?

Julius Caesar, III, 1, 148–150

Let's talk of graves, of worms, and epitaphs;
Make dust our paper, and with rainy eyes
Write sorrow on the bosom of the earth;
Let's choose executors and talk of wills:
And yet not so – for what can we bequeath
Save our deposed bodies to the ground?
Our lands, our lives, and all are Bolingbroke's,
And nothing can we call our own but death,
And that small model of the barren earth
Which serves as paste and cover to our bones,
For God's sake, let us sit upon the ground
And tell sad stories of the death of kings:
How some have been depos'd, some slain in war,
Some haunted by the ghosts they have depos'd,
Some poison'd by their wives, some sleeping kill'd;
All murder'd: for within the hollow crown
That rounds the mortal temples of a king
Keeps Death his court, and there the antick sits,
Scoffing his state and grinning at his pomp;
Allowing him a breath, a little scene,
To monarchize, be fear'd, and kill with looks,
Infusing him with self and vain conceit
As if this flesh which walls about our life
Were brass impregnable; and humour'd thus
Comes at the last, and with a little pin
Bores through his castle wall, and farewell king!

Richard II, III, 2, 145–170

But here there arises this irrepressible problem:
SALISBURY. My liege! my lord! But now a king, now thus.
PRINCE HENRY. Even so must I run on, and even so stop.
   What surety of the world, what hope, what stay,
   When this was now a king, and now is clay?

King John, V, 7, 66–69

*A question that raises a doubt about the meaning of history, for if
everything is equally corrupt and destined to end in dust, what can
be the significance of the 'human enterprise'? The first answer is
that of the moralist:*
Pride went before, ambition follows him.

While these do labour for their own preferment,
Behoves it us to labour for the realm.

Henry VI, Part 2, I, 1, 181–183

'Je maintiendrai.' Kings pass, but the nation remains:
The ripest fruit first falls, and so doth he.
His time is spent; our pilgrimage must be.

Richard II, II, 1, 154–155

*and since it survives every catastrophe, the nation must contain a
principle which it is history's mission to fulfill, a profound presence
which exists both in the community and the individual.*
There is a mystery – with whom relation
Durst never meddle – in the soul of state,
Which hath an operation more divine
Than breath or pen can give expression to.

Troilus and Cressida, III, 3, 202–205

There is a history in all men's lives,
Figuring the nature of the times deceas'd;
The which observ'd, a man may prophesy,
With a near aim, of the main chance of things
As yet not come to life, which in their seeds
And weak beginnings lie intreasured.

Henry IV, Part 2, III, 1, 80–85

*Which is to say that Shakespeare is confident that virtue will
prevail over corruption, light over darkness.*
For though usurpers sway the rule awhile,
Yet heavens are just, and time suppresseth wrongs.

Henry VI, Part 3, III, 3, 76–77

Does this mean that men must resign themselves to waiting? No, for
There is a tide in the affairs of men,
Which, taken at the flood, leads on to fortune;
Omitted, all the voyage of their life
Is bound in shallows and in miseries.

Julius Caesar, IV, 3, 217–220

*Thus men must strive for their own greatness by working for the
greatness of their country, sacrificing egoism to the general welfare:*
Look on thy country, look on fertile France,
And see the cities and the towns defac'd
By wasting ruin of the cruel foe.
As looks the mother on her lowly babe
When death doth close his tender dying eyes,

See, see the pining malady of France;
Behold the wounds, the most unnatural wounds,
Which thou thyself has giv'n her woeful breast.
O! turn thy edged sword another way;
Strike those that hurt, and hurt not those that help.
One drop of blood drawn from thy country's bosom,
Should grieve thee more than streams of foreign gore:
Return thee therefore, with a flood of tears,
And wash away thy country's stained spots.

Henry VI, Part 1, III, 3, 44–57

Thus, far from conforming to the chauvinism of so many Elizabethans, Shakespeare's patriotism embraces all nations, for he is convinced that the order he dreams of is dependent on world peace.

KING HENRY. Have you perus'd the letters from the pope,
    The emperor, and the Earl of Armagnac?
GLOUCESTER. I have, my lord; and their intent is this:
    They humbly sue unto your excellence
    To have a godly peace concluded of
    Between the realms of England and of France.
KING HENRY. How doth your Grace affect the motion?
GLOUCESTER. Well, my good lord; and as the only means
    To stop effusion of our Christian blood,
    And stablish quietness on every side.
KING HENRY. Ay, marry, uncle; for I always thought
    It was both impious and unnatural
    That such immanity and bloody strife
    Should reign among professors of one faith.

Henry VI, Part 1, V, 1, 1–14

And Shakespeare, after having portrayed the ambition of the mighty, the misery of the people, revolt, war, the nation's power, finally glorifies the harmony of men and gives us both the example and gauge of this alliance in the marriage of Henry V and Katherine of Valois.

Take her, fair son; and from her blood raise up
Issue to me; that the contending kingdoms
Of France and England, whose very shores look pale
With envy of each other's happiness,
May cease their hatred, and this dear conjunction
Plant neighborhood and Christian-like accord
In their sweet bosoms, that never war advance
His bleeding sword 'twixt England and fair France.

Henry V, V, 2, 376–383

153

Evil

The scourges that endlessly afflict nature, men, and nations finally lead Shakespeare to formulate the major problem of his theatre: evil, that enormous evil to which the initial reaction is despair.

> Lechery, lechery; still, wars and lechery:
> nothing else holds fashion.
>
> *Troilus and Cressida*, V, 2, 192–194

Such is the end of a slow but inexorable fall.

> I see, the jewel best enamelled
> Will lose his beauty; and though gold bides still
> That others touch, yet often touching will
> Wear gold; and no man that hath a name,
> By falsehood and corruption doth it shame.
>
> *The Comedy of Errors*, II, 1, 109–113

This falsehood and corruption are generally concealed, with the result that a perfidious dissimilarity reigns between appearance and reality.

> Mark you this, Bassanio,
> The devil can cite Scripture for his purpose.
> An evil soul, producing holy witness,
> Is like a villain with a smiling cheek,
> A goodly apple rotten at the heart:
> O what a goodly outside falsehood hath!
>
> *The Merchant of Venice*, I, 3, 98–103

This is a theme to which Shakespeare returns again and again, in various guises, from the comedies to the tragedies. It is not enough to say that it intrigued him; he was literally obsessed by it.

> So may the outward shows be least themselves:
> The world is still deceiv'd with ornament.
> In law, what plea so tainted and corrupt
> But, being season'd with a gracious voice,

155

Obscures the show of evil? In religion,
What damned error, but some sober brow
Will bless it and approve it with a text,
Hiding the grossness with fair ornament?
There is no vice so simple but assumes
Some mark of virtue on his outward parts.
How many cowards, whose hearts are all as false
As stairs of sand, wear yet upon their chins
The beards of Hercules and frowning Mars,
Who, inward search'd, have livers white as milk;
And these assume but valour's excrement
To render them redoubted! Look on beauty,
And you shall see 'tis purchas'd by the weight;
Which therein works a miracle in nature,
Making them lightest that wear most of it...
Thus ornament is but the guiled shore
To a most dangerous sea; the beauteous scarf
Veiling an Indian beauty; in a word,
The seeming truth which cunning times put on
To entrap the wisest. Therefore, thou gaudy gold,
Hard food for Midas, I will none of thee.

The Merchant of Venice, III, 2, 73–102

But if all is falsehood, all is danger.

I wonder men dare trust themselves with men:
Methinks they should invite them without knives;
Good for their meat, and safer for their lives.
There's much example for't; the fellow that
Sits next him now, parts bread with him, and pledges
The breath of him in a divided draught,
Is the readiest to kill him: 't has been prov'd.
If I were a huge man, I would fear to drink at meals;
Lest they should spy my wind-pipe's dangerous notes:
Great men should drink with harness on their throats.

Timon of Athens, I, 2, 45–54

Here is why we are always at the mercy of the unexpected.

And danger, like an ague, subtly taints
Even then when we sit idly in the sun.

Troilus and Cressida, III, 3, 233–234

This is the well-known phenomenon of being 'possessed'.

Five fiends have been in poor Tom at once;

of lust, as Obidicut; Hobbididance, prince
of dumbness; Mahu, of stealing; Modo, of
murder; and Flibbertigibbet, of mopping and
mowing; who since possesses chambermaids and
waiting women. So, bless thee, master!

King Lear, IV, 1, 59–64

Then follows the slow, dreadful martyrdom of thought.
Between the acting of a dreadful thing
And the first motion, all the interim is
Like a phantasma, or a hideous dream:
The genius and the mortal instruments
Are then in council; and the state of man,
Like to a little kingdom, suffers then
The nature of an insurrection.

Julius Caesar, II, 1, 63–69

*And what tends to freeze all resistance even more is the absolutely
arbitrary nature of the process.*
Some rise by sin, and some by virtue fall:
Some run from brakes of ice, and answer none,
And some condemned for a fault alone.

Measure For Measure, II, 1, 38–40

*Henceforth who can say he is unscathed? And how can we tell a
saint from a scoundrel?*
Thou rascal beadle, hold thy bloody hand!
Why dost thou lash that whore? Strip thine own back;
Thou hotly lust'st to use her in that kind
For which thou whipp'st her. The userer hangs the cozener.
Through tatter'd clothes small vices do appear;
Robes and furr'd gowns hide all. Plate sin with gold,
And the strong lance of justice hurtless breaks;
Arm it in rags, a pigmy's straw doth pierce it.
None does offend, none, I say none...

King Lear, IV, 6, 165–173

*None... for when a man is possessed to this degree he is nothing
more than the instrument of an evil which he can neither comprehend
nor cope with.*
As flies to wanton boys, are we to the gods.

Ibid., IV, 1, 36

157

As a matter of fact, it seems that for Shakespeare evil is unfathomable, infinite, so much so that the zeal of certain madmen has a quasi-comical element of grandiloquence about it.

LUCIUS. Art thou not sorry for these heinous deeds?
AARON. Ay, that I had not done a thousand more.
    Even now I curse the day, and yet, I think,
    Few come within the compass of my curse,
    Wherein I did not some notorious ill:
    As kill a man, or else devise his death;
    Ravish a maid, or plot the way to do it;
    Accuse some innocent, and forswear myself;
    Set deadly enmity between two friends;
    Make poor men's cattle break their necks;
    Set fire on barns and hay-stacks in the night,
    And bid the owners quench them with their tears,
    Oft have I digg'd up dead men from their graves,
    And set them upright at their dear friends' doors,
    Even when their sorrows almost were forgot;
    ...Tut! I have done a thousand dreadful things
    As willingly as one would kill a fly,
    And nothing grieves me heartily indeed
    But that I cannot do ten thousand more.
                        Titus Andronicus, V, 1, 123–144

But in flouting the laws of nature, crime delivers the criminal to his own fate.
    Had I but died an hour before this chance
    I had liv'd a blessed time; for, from this instant,
    There's nothing serious in mortality,
    All is but toys; renown and grace is dead,
    The wine of life is drawn, and the mere lees
    Is left this vault to brag of.
                            Macbeth, II, 3, 98–103

Ineluctably, crime begets crime.
                    But I am in
    So far in blood, that sin will pluck on sin:
    Tear-falling pity dwells not in this eye.
                         Richard III, IV, 2, 63–65

And the worst punishment is self punishment – remorse – which gnaws at the soul to the point of madness.
    Out, damned spot! out, I say! One;

two: why, then, 'tis time to do't. Hell is murky!...
Here's the smell of blood still:
All the perfumes of Arabia will not sweeten this
little hand. Oh! oh! oh!

Macbeth, V, 1, 38–57

Give me another horse! bind up my wounds!
Have mercy, Jesu! Soft! I did but dream.
O coward conscience, how dost thou afflict me!
The lights turn blue. It is now dead midnight.
Cold fearful drops stand on my trembling flesh.
What! Do I fear myself?...

Richard III, V, 3, 178–183

And from then on,
Better be with the dead,
Whom we, to gain our peace, have sent to peace,
Than on the torture of the mind to lie
In restless ecstasy.

Macbeth, III, 2, 19–22

There is always the solution of repentance, but alas...
Pray can I not,
Though inclination be as sharp as will:
My stronger guilt defeats my strong intent;
And, like a man to double business bound,
I stand in pause where I shall first begin,
And both neglect...
O wretched state! O bosom black as death!
O limed soul, that struggling to be free
Art more engaged!

Hamlet, III, 3, 38–69

*The drama of the damned is that of no longer caring whether or not
he is saved.*
I have almost forgot the taste of fears.
The time has been my senses would have cool'd
To hear a night-shriek, and my fell of hair
Would at a dismal treatise rouse and stir
As life were in't. I have supp'd full with horrors;
Direness, familiar to my slaughterous thoughts,
Cannot once start me.

Macbeth, V, 5, 9–15

Punishment's logic would that we might perish by the act through which we were raised.

> The gods are just, and of our pleasant vices
> Make instruments to plague us.
>
> *King Lear*, V, 3, 172–173

> Bloody thou art, bloody will be thy end;
> Shame serves thy life and doth thy death attend.
>
> *Richard III*, IV, 4, 195–196

But this atonement wrought by justice aims above all at destroying evil by evil, by drying up the springs.

> Hear, nature, hear! dear goddess hear!
> Suspend thy purpose, if thou didst intend
> To make this creature fruitful!
> Into her womb convey sterility!
> Dry up in her the organs of increase,
> And from her derogate body never spring
> A babe to honour her! If she must teem,
> Create her child of spleen, that it may live
> And be a thwart disnatur'd torment to her!
> Let it stamp wrinkles in her brow of youth,
> With cadent tears fret channels in her cheeks,
> Turn all her mother's pains and benefits
> To laughter and contempt, that she may feel
> How sharper than a serpent's tooth it is
> To have a thankless child!
>
> *King Lear*, I, 4, 299–313

These imprecations may seem naive to us, but for Shakespeare they obviously have a transcendental significance.

> BUCKINGHAM. Curses never pass the lips of those that breathe them in the air.
> QUEEN MARGARET. I will not think but they ascend the sky,
> And there awake God's gentle-sleeping peace.
>
> *Richard III*, I, 3, 285–288

When evil has reached its extreme limit it can only regress. It provokes a sort of divine revolt, a virtuous force which topples it.

> Things at the worst will cease, or else climb upward
> To what they were before.
>
> *Macbeth*, IV, 2, 24–25

But thus: if powers divine
Behold our human actions, as they do,
I doubt not then but innocence shall make
False accusation blush, and tyranny
Tremble at patience.

The Winter's Tale, III, 2, 29-33

*But such is tragedy's magnanimity that the guilty, in falling, achieve
a superhuman peace.*

And, when I am forgotten, as I shall be,
And sleep in dull cold marble, where no mention
Of me more must be heard of, say, I taught thee
Say, Wolsey, that once trod the ways of glory,
And sounded all the depths and shoals of honour,
Found thee a way, out of his wrack, to rise in.

Henry VIII, III, 2, 433–438

And once again Shakespeare concludes with an invocation to harmony:

The web of our life is of a mingled yarn, good
and ill together: our virtues would be proud if
our faults whipped them not; and our crimes
would despair if they were not cherished by our virtues.

All's Well That Ends Well, IV, 3, 83–87

Thus man, 'neither angel nor beast', should be slow to condemn:

It is a heretic that makes the fire,
Not she which burns in't.

The Winter's Tale, II, 3, 114–115

and finally learn to treat his fellow men with charity:

How would you be,
If He, which is the top of judgment, should
But judge you as you are? O! think on that,
And mercy then will breathe within your lips,
Like man made new.

Measure for Measure, II, 2, 75–79

Death

There is however one evil that none can avoid, and Shakespeare never stops reminding us of it: death.

But kings and mightiest potentates must die,
For that's the end of human misery.

Henry VI, Part 1, III, 2, 136–137

A condition common to all, of course, but yet how terrifying when you think about it.

We are such stuff
As dreams are made on, and our little life
Is rounded with a sleep.

The Tempest, IV, 1, 156–158

'To die, to sleep': two absences that seem so analogous to Shakespeare that we can, in this life, anticipate the other.

No, no, my dream was lengthen'd after life;
O! then began the tempest to my soul.
I passed, methought, the melancholy flood,
With that grim ferryman which poets write of,
Unto the kingdom of perpetual night.

Richard III, I, 4, 43–47

And, since they partake of death, dreams have the power of announcing its coming to us. Dreams, like nature's calamities, are a herald:

Come, Hector, come; go back:
The wife hath dream'd; they mother hath had visions;
Cassandra doth forsee; and I myself
Am like a prophet suddenly enrapt,
To tell thee that this day is ominous.

Troilus and Cressida, V, 3, 62–66

163

Orson Welles in Othello.

Thus there is a world of death, full of dreams, signs, secrets, and there are contacts between this world and ours that some people have the gift of perceiving.

SOOTHSAYER. Beware the ides of March.

CAESAR. What man is that?

BRUTUS. A soothsayer bids you beware the ides of March.

Julius Caesar, I, 2, 18–19

Perhaps it is this omniscience that makes death so desirable for the wretched.

Death, death: O, amiable lovely death!
Thou odiferous stench! sound rottenness!
Arise forth from the couch of lasting night,
Thou hate and terror to prosperity,
And I will kiss thy detestable bones,
And put my eyeballs in thy vaulty brows,
And ring these fingers with thy household worms,
And stop this gap of breath with fulsome dust,
And be a carrion monster like thyself:
Come, grin on me; and I will think thou smil'st
And buss thee as thy wife! Misery's love,
O! come to me.

King John, III, 4, 25–36

But it is also because death puts an end to our earthly troubles that the poet calls it 'comforting.'

Here lurks no treason, here no envy swells,
Here grow no damned drugs, here are no storms,
No noise, but silence and eternal sleep.

Titus Andronicus, I, 1, 153–155

Lovers yearn for this same repose. Separated here on earth, they dream of being united in another world. The tomb becomes their marriage bed.

Here will I remain
With worms that are thy chambermaids; O! here
Will I set up my everlasting rest,
And shake the yoke of inauspicious stars
From this world-wearied flesh. Eyes, look your last!
Arms, take your last embrace! and lips, O you
The doors of breath, seal with a righteous kiss
A dateless bargain to engrossing death!
Come, bitter conduct, come, unsavory guide!
Thou desperate pilot, now at once run on

The dashing rocks thy sea-sick weary bark!
Here's to my love! *(Drinks)* O true apothecary!
Thy drugs are quick. Thus with a kiss I die.

Romeo and Juliet, V, 3, 108–120

And finally, it is because death is the supreme atonement that it appeals to those enamored of justice.

Cold, cold, my girl!
Even like thy chastity.
O cursed, cursed slave! Whip me, ye devils,
From the possession of this heavenly sight!
Blow me about in winds! roast me in sulphur!
Wash me in steep-down gulfs of liquid fire!
O Desdemona! Desdemona! dead!

Othello, V, 2, 274–280

Nevertheless, all these reasons, however pertinent they may be, cannot bring man to leave this life of his own free will.

ABHORSON. Sirrah, bring Barnardine hither.

POMPEY. Master Barnardine! you must rise and be hanged, Master Barnardine.

ABHORSON. What ho! Barnardine!

BARNARDINE (Within). A pox o' your throats! Who makes that noise there? What are you?

POMPEY. Your friends, sir; the hangman. You must be so good, sir, to rise and be put to death.

BARNARDINE (Within). Away! you rogue, away! I am sleepy.

ABHORSON. Tell him he must awake, and that quickly too.

POMPEY. Pray, Master Barnardine, awake till you are executed, and sleep afterwards.

ABHORSON. Go in to him, and fetch him out.

POMPEY. He is coming, sir, he is coming; I hear his straw rustle.

ABHORSON. Is the axe upon the block, sirrah?

POMPEY. Very ready, sir. (Enter Barnardine)

BARNARDINE. How now, Abhorson! what's the news with you?

ABHORSON. Truly, sir, I would desire you to clap into your prayers; for, look you, the warrant's come.

BARNARDINE. You rogue, I have been drinking all night; I am not fitted for't.

POMPEY. O, the better, sir; for he that drinks all night, and is hang'd betimes in the morning, may sleep the sounder all the next day.

ABHORSON. Look you, sir; here comes your ghostly father:
do we jest now, think you?

Enter DUKE, disguised as a monk

DUKE. Sir, induced by my charity, and hearing how hastily
you are to depart, I come to advise you, comfort you, and
pray with you.

BERNARDINE. Friar, not I; I have been drinking hard all night,
and I will have more time to prepare me, or they shall beat
out my brains with billets. I will not consent to die this
day, that's certain.

DUKE. O, sir, you must; and therefore, I beseech you look
forward on the journey you shall go.

BERNARDINE. I swear I will not die today for any man's
persuasion.

DUKE. But hear you.

BERNARDINE. Not a word: if you have anything to say to me,
come to my ward; for thence will not I today.

Measure For Measure, IV, 3, 22–70

*For death remains the great enigma. Does it open the doors of
heaven or nothingness for us? Shakespeare considers both possibilities, and leaves us to draw our own conclusions.*

FIRST GAOLER. Come, sir, are you ready for death?...

POSTHUMUS. I am merrier to die than thou art to live.

FIRST GAOLER. Indeed, sir, he that sleeps feels not the tooth-
ache; but a man that were to sleep your sleep, and a
hangman to help him to bed, I think he would change
places with his officer; for look you, sir, you know not
which way you shall go...

POSTHUMUS. I tell thee, fellow, there are none want eyes to
direct them the way I am going but such as wink and will
not use them.

FIRST GAOLER. What an infinite mock is this, that a man
should have the best use of eyes to see the way of blindness!
I am sure hanging's the way of winking.

Cymbeline, V, 4, 152–197

*And indeed it is this final doubt that makes us question the very
meaning of our life and our acts.*

To be, or not to be; that is the question:
Whether 'tis nobler in the mind to suffer
The slings and arrows of outrageous fortune,
Or to take arms against a sea of troubles,

166

And by opposing end them? To die, to sleep;
No more; and, by a sleep to say we end
The heart-ache and the thousand natural shocks
That flesh is heir to, 'tis a consummation
Devoutly to be wish'd. To die, to sleep;
To sleep: perchance to dream; ay, there's the rub;
For in that sleep of death what dreams may come
When we have shuffled off this mortal coil,
Must give us pause. There's the respect
That makes calamity of so long life;
For who would bear the whips and scorns of time,
The oppressor's wrong, the proud man's contumely,

Then is my deede to my most painted word :
O heauy burthen.

Enter Hamlet,

Pol. I heare him comming, with-draw my Lord.
Ham. To be, or not to be, that is the question,
Whether tis nobler in the minde *to* suffer
The slings and arrowes of outragious fortune,
Or to take Armes against a sea of troubles,
And by opposing, end them, to die to sleepe
No more, and by a sleepe, to say we end
The hart-ake, and the thousand naturall shocks
That flesh is heire to; tis a consumation
Deuoutly to be wisht to die to sleepe,
To sleepe, perchance to dreame, I there's the rub,
For in that sleepe of death what dreames may come
When we haue shuffled off this mortall coyle
Must giue vs pause, there's the respect
That makes calamitie of so long life:
For who would beare the whips and scornes of time,
Th'oppressors wrong, the proude mans contumely,
The pangs of despiz'd loue, the lawes delay,
The insolence of office, and the spurnes
That patient merrit of th'vnworthy takes,
When he himselfe might his quietas make
With a bare bodkin; who would fardels beare,
To grunt and sweat vnder a wearie life,
But that the dread of something after death,
The vndiscouer'd country, from whose borne

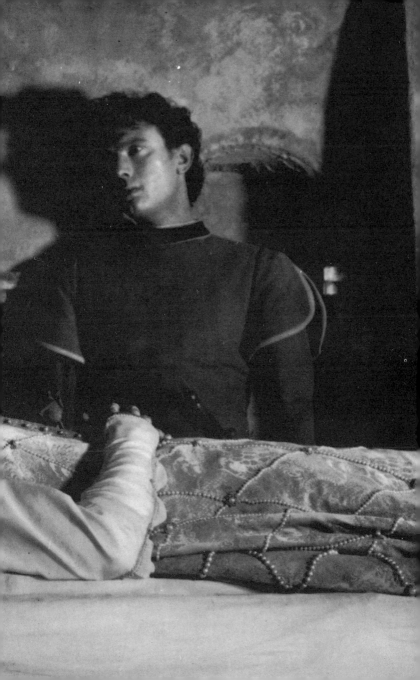

The pangs of dispriz'd love, the law's delay,
The insolence of office, and the spurns
That patient merit of the unworthy takes,
When he himself might his quietus make
With a bare bodkin? who would fardels bear
To grunt and sweat under a weary life,
But that the dread of something after death,
The undiscover'd country from whose bourn
No traveller returns, puzzles the will,
And makes us rather bear those ills we have
Than fly to others that we know not of?
Thus conscience does make cowards of us all;
And thus the native hue of resolution
Is sicklied o'er with the pale cast of thought,
And enterprises of great pith and moment
With this regard their currents turn awry,
And lose the name of action.

Hamlet, III, 1, 56–88

'*Make cowards of us all*', *for before this unknown we can only feel an almost physical horror.*

Ay, but to die, and go we know not where;
To lie in cold obstruction and to rot;
This sensible warm motion to become
A kneaded clod; and the delighted spirit
To bathe in fiery floods, or to reside
In thrilling region of thick-ribbed ice;
To be imprison'd in the viewless winds,
And blown with restless violence round about
The pendant worlds; or to be worse than worst
Of those that lawless and uncertain thoughts
Imagine howling: 'tis too horrible!
The weariest and most loathed worldly life
That age, ache, penury and imprisonment
Can lay on nature is a paradise
To what we fear of death.

Measure For Measure, III, 1, 116–130

Then death becomes absolute evil, the worst degradation that we have to submit to.

As thus: Alexander died, Alexander was buried, Alexander returneth into dust; the dust is earth; of earth we make loam,

170

and why of that loam, whereto he was converted, might they
not stop a beer-barrel?
Imperious Caesar dead and turned to clay,
Might stop a hole to keep the wind away.

Hamlet, V, 1, 230–236

*At the nadir of this fall, death will serve to slander life, by shaping
it in its image.*
And so, from hour to hour we ripe and ripe
And then from hour to hour we rot and rot.

As You Like It, II, 7, 26–27

To-morrow, and to-morrow, and to-morrow,
Creeps in this petty pace from day to day,
To the last syllable of recorded time;
And all our yesterdays have lighted fools
The way to dusty death. Out, out, brief candle!
Life's but a walking shadow, a poor player
That struts and frets his hour upon the stage
And then is heard no more; it is a tale
Told by an idiot, full of sound and fury,
Signifying nothing.

Macbeth, V, 5, 19–28

Thus death forces us to recognize that all is vanity:
For death remember'd should be like a mirror,
Who tells us life's but a breath, to trust it error.

Pericles, I, 1, 45–46

but at the same time it teaches us to rid ourselves of all illusions:
Join not with grief, fair woman, do not so,
To make my end too sudden: learn, good soul,
To think our former state a happy dream;
From which awak'd, the truth of what we are
Shows us but this. I am sworn brother, sweet,
To grim Necessity, and he and I
Will keep a league till death...
Our holy lives must win a new world's crown,
Which our profane hours here have stricken down.

Richard II, V, 1, 16–25

*Shakespeare offers us no 'diversion' from this death which lies in
wait for us. Rather, he urges us to accept lucidly*
Their going hence, even as their coming hither.
Ripeness is all.

King Lear, V, 2, 10–11

Be absolute for death; either death or life
Shall thereby be the sweeter.

Measure for Measure, III, 1, 5–6

*Pessimism? Rather wisdom and courage. We do not know what
fate holds in store for us 'when we have shuffled off this mortal coil';
all we know is that our body will return to the dust whence it has
come.*

Say to Athens,
Timon hath made his everlasting mansion
Upon the beached verge of the salt flood;
Who once a day with his embossed froth
The turbulent surge shall cover: thither come,
And let my grave-stone be your oracle.

Timon of Athens, V, 1, 219–224

But this universal rest blesses man with innocence and eternity...
Lie where the light foam of the sea may beat
Thy grave-stone daily.

Ibid., IV, 3, 381–382

And nature will slowly ennoble him with its wonders:
Full fathom five thy father lies;
Of his bones are coral made:
Those are pearls that were his eyes:
Nothing of him that doth fade,
But doth suffer a sea-change
Into something rich and strange.
Sea nymphs hourly ring his knell:
Hark! now I hear them, – ding-dong, bell.

The Tempest, I, 2, 394–401

To die is to become a part of the great poetry of the earth:
Death is now the phoenix' nest.

The Phoenix and the Turtle, 56

Poetry

> Time doth transfix the flourish set on youth
> And delves the parallels in beauty's brow,
> Feeds on the rarities of nature's truth,
> And nothing stands but for his scythe to mow:
> And yet to times in hope my verse shall stand,
> Praising thy worth, despite his cruel hand.
>
> *Sonnet LX*

This declaration, reiterated in Sonnets LXIII and LXV, teaches us that the poetic experience transcends and transfigures the experience of death, as sainthood transfigures life:

> My holy sir, none better knows than you
> How I have ever lov'd the life remov'd,
> And held in idle price to haunt assemblies
> Where youth, and cost, and witless bravery keeps.
>
> *Measure For Measure*, I, 3, 7–10

As a matter of fact Shakespeare has, on numerous occasions, depicted this or that king renouncing the courtly world for a life of meditation, an example that Shakespeare himself was to follow in his later years.

> I, thus neglecting worldly ends, all dedicated
> To closeness and the bettering of my mind
> With that, which, but by being so retir'd
> O'erpriz'd all popular rate.
>
> *The Tempest*, I, 2, 89–92

Like Descartes, Shakespeare believes that meditation will provide him with the key to the world. But, in contrast to the French philosopher, the science which Shakespeare here sings the praises

*of derives from magic – for example, the alchemist's medicine
capable of bringing the dead back to life:*

> 'Tis known I ever
> Have studied physic, through which secret art,
> By turning o'er authorities, I have –
> Together with my practice – made familiar
> To me and to my aid the blest infusions
> That dwell in vegètives, in metals, stones;
> And can speak of the disturbances
> That nature works, and of her cures; which doth give me
> A more content in course of true delight
> Than to be thirsty after tottering honour,
> Or tie my treasure up in silken bags,
> To please the fool and death.

Pericles, III, 2, 31–42

*Even aside from these speculations, man would find still more
'true joys' in a prison cell than in cities or palaces.*

> Come, let's away to prison:
> We two alone will sing like birds i' the cage:
> When thou dost ask me blessing, I'll kneel down
> And ask of thee forgiveness: so we'll live,
> And pray, and sing, and tell old tales, and laugh
> At gilded butterflies, and hear poor rogues
> Talk of court news; and we'll talk with them too,
> Who loses and who wins; who's in, who's out;
> And take upon's the mystery of things,
> As if we were God's spies: and we'll wear out,
> In a wall'd prison, packs and sets of great ones
> That ebb and flow by the moon.

King Lear, V, 3, 8–19

*However, though retreat may be all right for wise men, it is too
contrary to our normal make-up to accept without considerable
thought.*

> Whether, if you yield not to your father's choice,
> You can endure the livery of a nun,
> For aye to be in shady cloister mew'd,
> To live a barren sister all your life,
> Chanting faint hymns to the cold fruitless moon.
> Thrice blessed they that master so their blood,
> To undergo such maiden pilgrimage;
> But earthlier happy is the rose distill'd,

Than that which withering on the virgin thorn
Grows, lives, and dies, in single blessedness.

A Midsummer Night's Dream, I, 1, 69–79

And against this temptation of a bookish retreat, Shakespeare makes himself the advocate of life,

Why, all delights are vain; but that most vain
Which, with pain purchas'd doth inherit pain:
As, painfully to pore upon a book,
To seek the light of truth; while truth the while
Doth falsely blind the eyesight of his look...
Small have continual plodders ever won,
Save base authority from others' books.
These earthly godfathers of heaven's lights
That give a name to every fixed star,
Have no more profit of their shining nights
Than those that walk and wot not what they are.
Too much to know is to know nought but fame...

Love's Labour's Lost, I, 1, 72–93

and preaches, rather than this false knowledge, poetry, which is the relationship to be discovered between man and the universe:

Why should proud summer boast
Before the birds have any cause to sing?
Why should I joy in an abortive birth?
At Christmas I no more desire a rose
Than wish a snow in May's new-fangled mirth;
But like of each thing that in season grows.

Ibid., I, 1, 102–107

But no one may attain this wisdom unless he first divests himself of mediocre values.

I hold it ever,
Virtue and cunning were endowments greater
Than nobleness and riches; careless heirs
May the two latter darken and expend,
But immortality attends the former,
Making a man a god.

Pericles, III, 2, 26–31

All true poetry must have a moral basis, on which its sincerity depends.

He, who the sword of heaven will bear
Should be as holy as severe;

Pattern in himself to know,
Grace to stand, and virtue go;
More nor less to others paying
Than by self offences weighing.

Measure For Measure, III, 2, 283–288

And what are the cardinal virtues which will assure this 'authentic life'? Above all, charity, the mother of leniency and love:
Well, believe this,
No ceremony that to great ones 'longs,
Not the king's crown, nor the deputed sword,
The marshal's truncheon, nor the judge's robe,
Become them with one half so good a grace
As mercy does.

Ibid., II, 2, 58–63

For charity itself fulfils the law;
And who can sever love from charity?

Love's Labour's Lost, IV, 3, 364–365

Thus, on the threshold of the marvelous,
Pardon's the word to all.

Cymbeline, V, 5, 423

Nature itself sets us the example:
Some say that ever 'gainst that season comes
Wherein our Saviour's birth is celebrated,
The bird of dawning singeth all night long;
And then, they say, no spirit can walk abroad;
The nights are wholesome; then no planets strike,
No fairy takes, nor witch hath power to charm,
So hallow'd and so gracious is the time.

Hamlet, I, 1, 158–164

More than one of Shakespeare's heroes has already had a taste of this purity. Was it not in Iachimo's amazement in the presence of the sleeping Imogen?
The crickets sing, and man's o'erlabour'd sense
Repairs itself by rest. Our Tarquin thus
Did softly press the rushes ere he waken'd
The chastity he wounded. Cytherea,
How bravely thou becom'st thy bed! fresh lily,
And whiter than the sheets! That I might touch!
But kiss: one kiss! Rubies unparagon'd,
How dearly they do't! 'Tis her breathing that

176

Perfumes the chamber thus; the flame of the taper
Bows toward her, and would under-peep her lids,
To see the enclosed lights, now canopied
Under these windows, white and azure lac'd
With blue of heaven's own tint.

Cymbeline, II, 2, 11–23

Thus it seems that, through the voice of Miranda, beauty can say to the poet:

You have often
Begun to tell me what I am, but stopp'd
And left me to a bootless inquisition,
Concluding, 'Stay; not yet.'

The Tempest, I, 2, 33–36

But the time has come, poetry establishes its reign on earth.

I' the commonwealth I would by contraries
Execute all things: for no kind of traffic
Would I admit; no name of magistrate;
Letters would not be known; riches, poverty,
And use of service, none; contract, succession,
Bourn, bound of land, tilth, vineyard, none;
No use of metal, corn, or wine, or oil;
No occupation; all men idle, all;
And women too, but innocent and pure;
No sovereignty... Treason, felony,
Sword, pike, knife, gun, or need of any engine,
Would I not have; but nature should bring forth,
Of its own kind, all foison, all abundance,
To feed my innocent people.

Ibid., II, 1, 154–171

A dream no doubt, but one whose secret can still be discerned in the innocence of childhood...

We were as twinn'd lambs that did frisk i' the sun,
And bleat the one at the other: what we chang'd
Was innocence for innocence; we knew not
The doctrine of ill-doing, no nor dream'd
That any did. Had we pursu'd that life,
And our weak spirits ne'er been higher rear'd
With stronger blood, we should have answer'd heaven
Boldly, 'not guilty'; the imposition clear'd
Hereditary ours.

The Winter's Tale, I, 2, 67–75

177

To find this innocence again is to find the meaning of nature again:
> O Prosperina!
> For the flowers now that frighted thou let'st fall
> From Dis's waggon! daffodils,
> That come before the swallow dares, and take
> The winds of March with beauty; violets dim,
> But sweeter than the lids of Juno's eyes
> Or Cytherea's breath; pale prime-roses
> That die unmarried, ere they can behold
> Bright Phoebus in his strength, a malady
> Most incident to maids; bold oxlips and
> The crown imperial; lilies of all kinds
> The flower-de-luce being one. O! these I lack
> To make you garlands of, and my sweet friend,
> To strew him o'er and o'er!

Ibid., IV, 3, 116–129

and to gain entrance into this enchanted world of elves and sprites and nymphs, the world of Queen Mab and her fairy offspring, of Titania and her sylphs, this dream kingdom from which no one, once he has found it, ever wishes to leave.

> FERDINAND. This is a most majestic vision, and
> Harmonious charmingly: May I be bold
> To think these spirits?
> PROSPERO. Spirits, which by mine art
> I have from their confines call'd to enact
> My present fancies.
> FERDINAND. Let me live here ever:
> So rare a wonder'd father and a wise,
> Makes this place paradise.

The Tempest, IV, 1, 118–124

It is as if man were recovering a lost secret, the happiness he had once known in Eden:

> Be not afeard: the isle is full of noises,
> Sounds and sweet airs, that give delight, and hurt not.
> Sometimes a thousand twangling instruments
> Will hum about my ears; and sometime voices,
> That, if I then had wak'd after long sleep,
> Will make me sleep again: and then, in dreaming,
> The clouds methought would open and show riches
> Ready to drop upon me; that, when I wak'd
> I cried to dream again.   *Ibid.*, III, 2, 147–154

Thus poetry is really the philosopher's stone. It opens a superior world to us, the world as it existed before man's fall.

> What seest thou else
> In the dark backward and abysm of time?
> If thou remember'st aught ere thou cams't here,
> How thou cam'st here, thou may'st.

Ibid., I, 2, 49–52

So it is that the poet can conclude on a note of both pride and humility:

> He that of greatest works is finisher
> Oft does them by the weakest minister:
> So holy writ in babes hath judgment shown,
> When judges have been babes; great floods have flown
> From simple sources; and great seas have dried
> When miracles have by the greatest been denied.

All's Well That Ends Well, II, 1, 139–144

Shakespeare poured forth his poetry into the heart of the universe. It charmed even the beasts and stones:

> Therefore the poet
> Did feign that Orpheus drew trees, stones, and floods;
> Since nought so stockish, hard, and full of rage,
> But music for the time doth change his nature.
> The man that hath no music in himself
> Nor is not mov'd with concord of sweet sounds,
> Is fit for treasons, stratagems, and spoils;
> The motions of his spirit are dull as night,
> And his affections dark as Erebus:
> Let no such man be trusted.

The Merchant of Venice, V, 1, 79–88

and initiated man to his own grandeur:

> How sweet the moonlight sleeps upon this bank!
> Here will we sit, and let the sounds of music
> Creep in our ears: soft stillness and the night
> Become the touches of sweet harmony.
> Sit, Jessica: look, how the floor of heaven
> Is thick inlaid with patines of bright gold:
> There's not the smallest orb which thou behold'st
> But in his motion like an angel sings,
> Still quiring to the young-eyed cherubins;
> Such harmony is in immortal souls;
> But, whilst this muddy vesture of decay

Doth grossly close it in, we cannot hear it.

Ibid., V, 1, 54–65

and led the poet to his supreme enigma:
Where should this music be? i' the air, or th' earth?
It sounds no more.

The Tempest, I, 2, 385–386

The work is accomplished. Shakespeare can close his book forever.
Ye elves of hills, brooks, standing lakes, and groves;
And ye, that on the sands with printless foot
Do chase the ebbing Neptune and do fly him
When he comes back; you demi-puppets, that
By moonshine do the green sour ringlets make
Whereof the ewe not bites; and you, whose pastime
Is to make midnight mushrooms; that rejoice
To hear the solemn curfew; by whose aid, –
Weak masters though ye be – I have bedimm'd
The noontide sun, call'd forth the mutinous winds,
And 'twixt the green sea and the azur'd vault
Set roaring war: to the dread-rattling thunder
Have I given fire and rifted Jove's stout oak
With his own bolt: the strong bas'd promontory
Have I made shake; and by the spurs pluck'd up
The pine and cedar: graves at my command
Have wak'd their sleepers, op'd, and let them forth
By my so potent art. But this rough magic
I here abjure; and, when I have requir'd
Some heavenly music, – which even now I do, –
To work mine end upon their senses that
This airy charm is for, I'll break my staff,
Bury it certain fathoms in the earth,
And deeper than did ever plummet sound,
I'll drown my book.

Ibid., V, 1, 33–57

Death can come, the poet pass away, but poetry itself remains and is ever renewed:
Hark! hark! the lark at heaven's gate sings.

Cymbeline, II, 3, 22

THE
TEMPEST.

Actus primus, Scena prima.

A tempestuous noise of Thunder and Lightning heard: Enter a Ship-master, and a Botes-waine.

Master.

BOte-swaine.

Botes. Heere Master : What cheere?

Mast. Good : Speake to th'Mariners : fall too't, yarely, or we run our selues a ground, bestirre, bestirre. *Exit.*

Enter Mariners.

Botes. Heigh my hearts, cheerely, cheerely my harts : yare, yare : Take in the toppe-sale : Tend to th'Masters whistle : Blow till thou burst thy winde, if roome enough.

Enter Alonso, Sebastian, Anthonio, Ferdinando, Gonzalo, and others.

Alon. Good Botefwaine haue care : where's the Master? Play the men.

Botes. I pray now keepe below.

Anth. Where is the Master, Boson?

Botes. Do you not heare him? you marre our labour, Keepe your Cabines : you do assist the storme.

Conz. Nay, good be patient.

Botes. When the Sea is : hence, what cares these roarers for the name of King? to Cabine; silence : trouble vs not.

Gon. Good, yet remember whom thou hast aboord.

Botes. None that I more loue then my selfe. You are a Counsellor, if you can command these Elements to silence, and worke the peace of the present, wee will not hand a rope more, vse your authoritie : If you cannot, giue thankes you haue liu'd so long, and make your selfe readie in your Cabine for the mischance of the houre, if it so hap. Cheerely good hearts : out of our way I say. *Exit.*

Gon. I haue great comfort from this fellow: methinks he hath no drowning marke vpon him, his complexion is perfect Gallowes : stand fast good Fate to his hanging, make the rope of his destiny our cable, for our owne doth little aduantage : If he be not borne to bee hang'd, our case is miserable. *Exit.*

Enter Botefwaine.

Botes. Downe with the top-Mast : yare, lower, lower, bring her to Try with Maine-course, *A plague*——
A cry within. *Enter Sebastian, Anthonio & Gonzalo.*

vpon this howling : they are lowder then the weather, or our office : yet againe? What do you heere? Shal we giue ore and drowne, haue you a minde to sinke?

Sebas. A poxe o'your throat, you bawling, blasphemous incharitable Dog.

Botes. Worke you then.

Anth. Hang cur, hang, you whoreson insolent Noysemaker, we are lesse afraid to be drownde, then thou art.

Gonz. I'le warrant him for drowning, though the Ship were no stronger then a Nutt-shell, and as leaky as an vnstaunched wench.

Botes. Lay her a hold, a hold, set her two courses off to Sea againe, lay her off.

Enter Mariners wet.

Mari. All lost, to prayers, to prayers, all lost.

Botes. What must our mouths be cold?

Gonz. The King, and Prince, at prayers, let's assist them, for our case is as theirs.

Sebas. I'am out of patience.

An. We are meerly cheated of our liues by drunkards, This wide-chopt-rascall, would thou mightst lye drowning the washing of ten Tides.

Gonz. Hee'l be hang'd yet, Though euery drop of water sweare against it, And gape at widst to glut him. *A confused noyse within.*

Mercy on vs.

We split, we split, Farewell my wife, and children, Farewell brother : we split, we split, we split.

Anth. Let's all sinke with' King

Seb. Let's take leaue of him. *Exit.*

Gonz. Now would I giue a thousand furlongs of Sea, for an Acre of barren ground : Long heath, Browne firrs, any thing ; the wills aboue be done, but I would faine dye a dry death. *Exit.*

Scena Secunda.

Enter Prospero and Miranda.

Mira. If by your Art (my deerest father) you haue Put the wild waters in this Rore; alay them : The skye it seemes would powre down stinking pitch, But that the Sea, mounting to th' welkins cheeke, Dashes the fire out. Oh! I haue suffered With those that I saw suffer : A braue vessell

A

(Who

Shakespeare and the Critics

That Shakespeare was the greatest dramatist of all times, and the greatest poet of modern times, few will contest today. Veritable shrines dedicated solely to the performance of his plays exist not only at Stratford-on-Avon, but also at Stratford, Ontario, and Stratford, Connecticut. His works have been translated into every language of the civilized world, and one can only guess at the staggering number of commentaries and criticisms both about the man and his work that have appeared during the more than three centuries since his death.

Understandably, the majority of Shakespearean criticism and research has been done by the poet's fellow-countrymen and by those countries of the world where English is the native tongue. This is not to disparage the many excellent Shakespearean studies that have been written in almost every country where translations of the poet's work are available, but the fact remains that no translation, however inspired, can hope to convey the full beauty of what was perhaps his supreme achievement: his unparalleled mastery of the English language.

In these pages, then, we shall offer a random sampling of commentaries and opinions culled primarily from English language sources, although a limited number of pertinent French and German quotations will be included, not only to indicate the poet's stature abroad, but to demonstrate the great disparity that has existed from age to age and writer to writer, ranging from Voltaire's remark about 'pearls in the dung heap' to Goethe's profound and perceptive exposition of Hamlet's nature and fate.

We have already seen that as early as 1598, when Shakespeare was still in his middle thirties, the critic Francis Meres compared him to Ovid, Plautus, and Seneca:

Orson Welles in Macbeth.

'As the soule of *Euphorbus* was thought to live in *Pythagoras:* so the sweete wittie soule of *Ovid* lives in mellifluous & hony-tongued Shakespeare... As *Plautus* and *Seneca* are accounted best for Comedy and Tragedy among the Latines, so *Shakespeare* among the English is the most excellent for both kinds for the stage....'

(Palladis Tamia)

One of the principal indications we have of the degree of Shakespeare's scholarship is to be found in Ben Jonson's famous ode which makes up part of the preliminary matter of the First Folio of 1623, one line of which reads: '*And though thou hadst small* Latin *and less* Greek.' In spite of this reflection, which many have taken to be a conscious or unconscious manifestation of Jonson's envy, the ode is filled with such eulogistic terms that one can scarcely doubt the sincerity of Jonson's admiration:

> *To draw no envy* [Shakespeare] *on thy name,*
> *Am I thus ample to thy Book and Fame:*
> *While I confess thy writings to be such*
> *As neither* Man *nor* Muse *can praise too much...*
> > *Soule of the Age!*
> *The applause! delight! the wonder of our Stage!...*
> *Thou art a Monument without a tomb,*
> *And art alive still while thy Book doth live*
> *And we have wits to read and praise to give.*

One of the few contemporary judgments on Shakespeare the man that has come down to us is that of Jonson who, a few years after the '*Sweet Swan of Avon*'s' death, said of him:

> I lov'd the man, and do honour his memory (on this side of Idolatry) as much as any. He was (indeed) honest, and of an open, and free nature: had an excellent Phantasie; brave notions, and gentle expressions.

Nicholas Rowe, who in 1709 published the first regular biography of Shakespeare, relates a pleasant and credible story that could well account for Jonson's 'near Idolatry' of Shakespeare. According to Rowe, it was Shakespeare who rescued Ben Jonson's comedy, *Every Man in His Humour*, from the hands of some supercilious and unperceptive members of the Globe company to whom it had been submitted, and, says Rowe, it was Shakespeare who later recommended Jonson to the public. Be that as it may, Shakespeare's name does appear first in the list of 'Principal Comedians' who acted in *Every Man in His Humour* when it was first performed in 1598.

A few years after the First Folio appeared, John Milton penned these panegyric lines:

> What needs my Shakespear for his honour'd bones,
> The labour of an age in pilèd Stones,
> Or that his hallow'd relics should be hid

Under a Stary-pointing *Pyramid?*
Dear Son of memory, great heir of Fame,
What need'st thou such weak witness of thy name?
Thou in our wonder and astonishment
Hast built thyself a live-long Monument.

(On Shakespeare, 1630)

Thus there seems little doubt that Shakespeare's contemporaries – or at least the more perceptive – did recognize the giant in their midst. But only time, which Shakespeare himself perceived as the great leveller, would prove during the next three and a quarter centuries how unique the giant really was. 'The stream of time,' said Dr. Johnson, 'which is continually washing the dissolute fabricks of other poets, passes without injury the adamant Shakespeare.' Of course there were detractors, men who, through envy, literary myopia, or the changing tastes of their era, found Shakespeare 'affected,' 'lacking in art,' or just plain 'dull.' But they are relatively few, and for the most part those writers and critics who have written about him vie with one another for the role of principal panegyrist, as the following examples will show:

Shakespeare, who many times has written better than any poet, in any language, is yet too far from writing wit always, or expressing that wit according to the dignity of the subject, that he writes, in many places, below the dullest writers of ours, or any precedent age. Never did any author precipitate himself from such height of thought to so low expressions, as he often does. He is the very Janus of poets; he wears almost everywhere two faces; and you have scarce begun to admire the one, ere you despise the other... Let us therefore admire the beauties and the height of Shakespeare, without falling after him into a carelessness, and, as I may call it, a lethargy of thought for whole scenes together.

(John Dryden, 1672)

If ever any author deserved the name of an original, it was Shakespeare. Homer himself drew not his art so immediately from the fountains of Nature; it proceeded thro' Aegyptian strainers and channels, and came to him not without some tincture of the learning, or some cast of the models, of those before him. The poetry of Shakespeare was inspiration indeed: he is not so much an imitator, as an instrument, of Nature; and 'tis not so just to say that he speaks from her, as that she speaks thro' him. His characters are so much Nature herself that 'tis a sort of injury to call them by so distant a name as copies of her.

(Alexander Pope, 1725)

This therefore is the praise of Shakespeare, that his drama is the mirror of life; that he who has mazed his imagination, in following the phantoms which other writers raise up before him, may here be

185

cured of his delirious ecstasies, by reading human sentiments in human language; by scenes from which a hermit may estimate the transactions of the world, and a confessor predict the progress of the passions. *(Dr. Samuel Johnson)*

Shakespeare, whom the English take for a Sophocles, flourished at about the same time as Lope de Vega; he created a theater; his was a genius both fertile and forceful, natural and sublime, but he was completely lacking in good taste and had no respect whatever for the rules. *(Voltaire, 1734)*

The French have always been preoccupied with the 'rules' that Voltaire mentions – perhaps over preoccupied – with the result that, while recognizing Shakespeare's genius, they have tended to treat him like a strange, almost abnormal phenomenon of the literary world. He shocks their Cartesian minds, their sense of order and good taste.

For a thing to be beautiful according to the rules of taste, it must be elegant, polished, worked without seeming to be; for it to be a work of genius, it must sometimes seem neglected, have something irregular, abrupt and savage about it. The sublime and genius shine in Shakespeare like flashes in a long night, and Racine is always beautiful. *(Diderot, 1757)*

Some twenty years after Diderot's comment, and more than forty years after his earlier remarks about Shakespeare, Voltaire returned to the subject in a letter to the Count of Argental in which he inveighed against the uncouth English poet and blamed himself for having introduced the monster into France:

And the horrible part about it is that the monster has his admirers in France; and what is even worse and more unforgiveable, it was I who first showed the French the few pearls I had found in his enormous dung heap. Little did I suspect that I would one day serve to trample underfoot the crowns of Racine and Corneille and help to place them on the brow of a barbaric actor.

(Voltaire, 1776)

There are beauties of the first order to be found in Shakespeare, relating to every country and every period of time. His faults are those which belonged to the times in which he lived... One of the greatest faults which Shakespeare can be accused of, is his want of simplicity in the intervals of his sublime passages. When he is not exalted, he is affected; he wanted the act of sustaining himself, that is to say, of being natural in his scenes of transition, as he was in the grand movements of the soul. *(Mme. de Staël, 1800)*

The striking peculiarity of Shakespeare's mind was its generic quality, its power of communication with all other minds... He not only had in himself the germs of every faculty and feeling, but he could follow them by anticipation, intuitively, into all their conceivable ramifications, through every change of fortune or conflict of passions or turn of thought. He had 'a mind reflecting ages past' and present: – all the people that ever lived are there.

(*William Hazlitt*, 1817)

Shakespeare, no mere child of nature; no automaton of genius; no passive vehicle of inspiration possessed by the spirit, not possessing it; first studied patiently, meditated deeply, understood minutely, till knowledge, become habitual and intuitive, wedded itself to his habitual feelings, and at length gave birth to that stupendous power, by which he stands alone, with no equal or second in his own class. (*Samuel Taylor Coleridge*, 1817)

At every new accession of information, after every successful exercise of meditation, and every fresh presentation of experience, I have unfailingly discovered a proportionate increase of wisdom and intuition in Shakespeare.
Merciful, wonder-making Heaven! What a man was this Shakespeare! Myriad-minded, indeed he was!

(*Samuel Taylor Coleridge*, 1818)

O mighty poet, thy works are not as those of other men, simply and merely great works of art; but are also like the phenomena of nature, like the sun and the sea, the stars and the flowers; like frost and snow, rain and dew, hail-storm and thunder, which are to be studied with entire submission of our own faculties, and in the perfect faith that in them there can be no too much or too little, nothing useless or inert – but that, the farther we press our discoveries, the more we shall see proofs of design, and self-supporting arrangement where the careless eye had seen nothing but accident!

(*Thomas De Quincey*, 1823)

Even as Jesus Christ impressed the son of Hamonia, so am I impressed by William Shakespeare. I grow desperate when I reflect that after all he is an Englishman, belonging to that most odious nation which God in his anger created. (*Heinrich Heine*, 1838)

My admiration for Shakespeare increases every day. That man never is boring, and he is the most perfect image of nature. His is the book that suits me. (*Stendhal*, 1825)

Consider now, if they asked us, 'Will you give up your Indian Empire or your Shakespeare, you English; never have had any Indian Empire, or never have had any Shakespeare?'... Should not we be forced to answer: 'Indian Empire, or no Indian Empire; we cannot do without Shakespeare!' (*Thomas Carlyle*, 1840)

A rib of Shakespeare would have made a Milton, the same portion of Milton all poets born ever since. (*Walter Savage Landor*, 1846)

187

Now literature, philosophy and thought are Shakespearized. His mind is the horizon beyond which, at present, we do not see. Our ears are educated to music by his rhythm... Shakespeare is the only biographer of Shakespeare; and even he can tell nothing, except to the Shakespeare in us, that is, to our most apprehensive and sympathetic hour... He was a full man, who liked to talk; a brain exhaling thoughts and images, which, seeking vent, found the drama next at hand. Had he been less, we should have had to consider how well he filled his place, how good a dramatist he was, – and he is the best in the world.

(*Ralph Waldo Emerson*, 1856–76)

Superb and inimitable as all is, it is mostly an objective and physiological kind of power and beauty the soul finds in Shakespeare – a style supremely grand of the sort, but in my opinion stopping short of the grandest sort, at any rate for fulfilling and satisfying modern and democratic American purposes... The comedies are altogether non-acceptable to America and Democracy.

(*Walt Whitman*, 1888)

I never open my Shakespeare but I find myself wishing that there might be professorships established for the expounding of his works, as there used to be for those of Dante in Italy. There is nothing in all literature so stimulating and suggestive as the thought he seems to drop by chance, as if his hands were too full. Nothing so cheery as his humor; nothing that laps us in Elysium so quickly as the lovely images which he marries to the music of his verse. He is also a great master of rhetoric in teaching us what to follow, and sometimes quite as usefully what to avoid. I value him above all for this, that for those who know no language but their own, there is as much intellectual training to be got from the study of his works as that from the works of any, I almost had said all, of the great writers of antiquity.

(*James Russell Lowell*)

It is often said that we know nothing about Shakespeare the man. It seems to me there is no man about whom I know so much.

(*Alfred Austin*)

With the single exception of Homer, there is no eminent writer, not even Sir Walter Scott, whom I can despise so entirely as I despise Shakespeare when I measure my mind against his. The intensity of my impatience with him occasionally reaches such a pitch, that it would positively be a relief to me to dig him up and throw stones at him, knowing as I do how incapable he and his worshippers are of understanding any less obvious form of indignity.

(*George Bernard Shaw*)

There are two main categories of characters in Shakespeare: people of action and those who are irresolute, and in many of his plays he sets one against the other. And often the irresolute is the protagonist of the play, the very subject of which becomes the deterioration and progressive retreat of the hero before this other type who is better adapted to life. The former is often endowed with the most exquisite qualities; the latter is stronger because he is less scrupulous. This very often results in the sacrifice of the better characters.

(*André Gide*)

What did Shakespeare do? What did he add to the world's totality?... If he had never lived, things would be very much as they are... He added no idea, altered no idea, in the growing understanding of mankind.

(*H. G. Wells*)

While it is interesting to read what other men have had to say about Shakespeare, while their remarks and opinions can indeed add to our knowledge and appreciation of the world's greatest dramatist, one suspects that perhaps the most pertinent advice ever given by any commentary was made over three hundred years ago by Shakespeare's friends and first editors, John Heminge and Henry Condell:

His [Shakespeare's] mind and hand went together; and what he thought, he uttered with that easinesse that wee have scarse received from him a blot in his papers. But it is not our province, who onely gather his works and give them you, to praise him. It is yours that reade him. And there we hope, to your divers capacities, you will finde enough both to draw and hold you; for his wit can no more lie hid then it could be lost. Reade him, therefore; and againe and againe....

(*Introduction to the First Folio*)

and echoed by Dr. Johnson a hundred and fifty years later:

Let him that is yet unacquainted with the powers of Shakespeare, and who desires to feel the highest pleasure that the Drama can give, read every Play, from the first scene to the last, with utter negligence of all the commentators. When his fancy is once on the wing, let it not stoop to correction or explanation. When his attention is strongly engaged, let it disdain alike to turn aside in to the name of Theobald or Pope. Let him read on through integrity and corruption, let him preserve his comprehension of the dialogue, and his interest in the fable. And when the pleasures of novelty have ceased, let him attempt exactness and read the commentators.

A NOTE ON THE ILLUSTRATIONS

The documents illustrating this volume were gathered from the following sources:

The *Bibliothèque Nationale* in Paris: pp. 2, 11, 15, 17, 18, 19, 22, 24, 45, 51, 52, 58, 63, 64, 67, 70, 91, 103, 104, 116, 121, 123, 143, 146, 153, 167, 172.

The *National Portrait Gallery:* pp. 6, 7, 40, 60, 178.

The *British Museum:* pp. 8, 36, 69, 81, 118, 179.

The *London Museum:* pp. 13, 46–47, 56–57.

Shakespeare's Birthplace: pp. 30, 32–33, 34, 35, 37, 54, 73, 75, 76, 77, 112.

J. E. Bulloz, publisher: pp. 136, 159.

Giraudon: p. 29.

The illustrations appearing on pages 4, 118, 130, 140, 154, 162, 168–169, 186, are taken from the following films: *Richard III* (Laurence Olivier), *Hamlet* (Laurence Olivier), *Julius Caesar* (Mankiewicz), *Othello* (Orson Welles), *Romeo and Juliet* (Castellani), *Macbeth* (Orson Welles).

We would also like to express our gratitude to M. Miron Grindea, director of the magazine *Adam*, Mr. Martin Holmes of the *London Museum*, and to the librarians of the *British Museum*, the *Guildhall Library*, the *Public Record Office*, and the *National Portrait Gallery* for their invaluable help in the preparation of this volume.

191

Marlon Brando and Louis Calhern in Julius Caesar.

Make no Collection of it. Let him shew
His skill in the construction.

Luc. Philarmonus.

Sooth. Heere, my good Lord.

Luc. Read, and declare the meaning.

Reader.

WHen as a Lyons whelpe, st all to himselfe vnknowne, without seeking finde, and bee embrac'd by a peece of tender
Ayre: And when from a stately Cedar shal be lopt branches,
which being dead many yeares, shall after renue, bee ioynted to
the old Stocke, and freshly grow, then shall Posthumus end his
miseries, Britaine be fortunate, and flourish in Peace and Plen-
tie.

Thou *Leonatus* art the Lyons Whelpe,
The fit and apt Construction of thy name
Being *Leonatus*, doth import so much:
The peece of tender Ayre, thy vertuous Daughter,
Which we call *Mollis Aer*, and *Mollis Aer*
We terme it *Mulier*; which *Mulier* I diuine
Is this most constant Wife, who euen now
Answering the Letter of the Oracle,
Vnknowne to you vnsought, were clipt about
With this most tender Aire.

Cym. This hath some seeming.

Sooth. The lofty Cedar, Royall *Cymbeline*
Personates thee: And thy lopt Branches, point
Thy two Sonnes forth: who by *Belarius* stolne
For many yeares thought dead, are now reuiu'd
To the Maiesticke Cedar ioyn'd; whose Issue

Promises Britaine, Peace and Plenty.

Cym. Well,
My Peace we will begin: And *Caius Lucius*,
Although the Victor, we submit to *Cæsar*,
And to the Romane Empire; promising
To pay our wonted Tribute, from the which
We were disswaded by our wicked Queene,
Whom heauens in Iustice both on her, and hers,
Haue laid most heauy hand.

Sooth. The fingers of the Powres aboue, do tune
The harmony of this Peace : the Vision
Which I made knowne to *Lucius* ere the stroke
Of yet this scarse-cold-Battaile, at this instant
Is full accomplish'd. For the Romane Eagle
From South to West, on wing soaring aloft
Lessen'd her selfe, and in the Beames o'th'Sun
So vanish'd; which fore-shew'd our Princely Eagle
Th'Imperiall *Cæsar*, should againe vnite
His Fauour, with the Radiant *Cymbeline*,
Which shines heere in the West.

Cym. Laud we the Gods,
And let our crooked Smoakes climbe to their Nostrils
From our blest Altars. Publish we this Peace
To all our Subiects. Set we forward : Let
A Roman, and a Brittish Ensigne waue
Friendly together : so through *Luds-Towne* march,
And in the Temple of great Iupiter
Our Peace wee'l ratifie : Seale it with Feasts.
Set on there : Neuer was a Warre did cease
(Ere bloodie hands were wash'd) with such a Peace.

Exeunt.

FINIS.